AGING INTO POVERTY

THE **LOOMING CRISIS** FOR AMERICAN WOMEN

KATHY SHARP

ISBN: 979-8-9863294-0-6 (Paperback Edition)
ISBN: 979-8-9863294-1-3 (eBook)

To my mother Mary C. Mulhall
and to her devoted caregivers
Amanda Scott and Sue Kupihea

CONTENTS

INTRODUCTION

Our seniors deserve to age with love, support, and dignity, versus aging into poverty. My mother Mary was a college-educated professional woman who owned a home, an accounting practice, and had considerable savings. Yet when she died at the age of 94, she was in a Medicaid-sponsored bed in a nursing home. This was after spending her final years living in a trailer and receiving food stamps. In many ways, Mary was lucky. She had family and a supportive community. However, her final years were far from the resort-like pictures of aging adults we see in television ads for senior living.

As my mother neared the end of her life, I was sandwiched between the needs of my teen-aged children, my partner, my full-time job, and my responsibility of caring for my aging parent. There were very few resources to support women in my position. Identifying options available to support my mother and adapting as her health needs and financial picture changed proved to be a steep learning curve. I found that the social service safety net was badly frayed, if non-existent, and that the assistance to support my mother in the activities of daily living to enable her to live independently was incredibly expensive.

I am Mary's only daughter and took responsibility for helping her navigate the choices she faced as she aged. I am writing this book as a reflection on those difficult years. I wish I had the information then that I have now. Even with this knowledge, I may not have been able to change my mother's decisions; she was one stubborn lady. However, I would have liked to have been better prepared to present her with options. Maybe we could have gotten one step ahead of the changes she faced, instead of always being in a reactive mode. I'd like to think that if families have a better idea of what might be coming, and better understand the ins and outs of the health- and elder-care systems (particularly how they affect women as they age) then empowerment might slowly replace shock and heartache.

I am not alone—too many women my age in this country currently find themselves in the position I was in with my mother. I don't believe that my story, or my mother's story, is unique. Unfortunately, aging women in poverty is a fast-growing demographic. The U.S. Census Bureau's "Supplemental Poverty Measure" (SPM) estimates that 16 percent of women age 65 and older live at or below the poverty line![1] Among people ages 85 and older, 23 percent of women living alone were in poverty, compared with 9 percent of men living alone. These statistics are alarming. For minority and LGBTQ women, the numbers are even higher. Sadly, my mother was part of a growing demographic trend. In writing this book, I wanted to put her story into a larger context.

In chapter one, I recount the final decade of my mother's life as she transitioned from independent living to assisted living and ultimately skilled nursing. While my mother ended her life in poverty, senior care is big business in the United States. Large corporations aided by favorable tax structures create record profits for investors. Yet, the United States is the only industrialized county that does not have a comprehensive program of provisioning health care for our population, including our seniors.

Chapter two explores the history of the provisioning of senior care in the United States from early colonial times to the present day. It is interesting to follow the recurring discussions around what responsibility our society has to care for those who cannot care for themselves. This political and moral consideration is posed to each generation, with different decisions and solutions evolving over time. From village elders who auctioned off widows to the lowest bidding farmer, to the policy tradeoffs that left hundreds of thousands behind with the enactment of Medicaid and later Obamacare, America's privatized care system has long struggled to care for the poor, the old, and the sick.

In chapter three, we look at the women who struggle to meet their own needs while caring for dependent seniors. One of the constants in the discussion of caring for the elderly is that women are almost solely responsible for their care, either as paid caregivers or family members. In America, as high as 75 percent of caregivers, whether paid workers or unpaid family members, are women. Daughters step up twice as often as sons. By virtue of giving care, women put themselves at risk for falling into poverty themselves later in life. Elder care seems to be the final frontier for feminism.

In chapter four, we explore the programs that make up the frayed social safety net that's supposed to support the most vulnerable. From Meals on Wheels to IHSS and HEAP, there are many social programs designed to assist seniors in meeting their basic needs. However, this safety net is full of holes, challenging to navigate, and often exclusionary, leaving senior women (and those who care for them) at risk.

The book culminates with a look at what can be done, with chapter five taking on a solutions-centered approach. Acknowledging the gaps in public policy options, we find creative solutions for caring for the dependent elderly. From backyard cottages to family agreements and technology assists, these solutions can help families think outside of the box. We explore the key dimensions to be considered—housing, healthcare and autonomy—and make recommendations for maximizing the senior's experience in each of these areas.

The book concludes with a timeline for decision making and planning. In chronicling Mary's journey and my own learning curve, I hope to leave you with a bread-crumb trail to follow. There is no-one-size-fits-all approach, but there are key considerations and solutions.

COVID-19 drew our attention to a population that is frequently out of sight and out of mind: seniors in congregant living facilities. Early in the pandemic, the virus spread unchecked through nursing homes and senior facilities, causing death, and leaving vulnerable seniors locked in their rooms for months at a time. My hope is that now that the nation's attention has been focused on senior care, we can turn our attention to the plight of women like Mary and avert our continuing crisis of women aging into poverty.

CHAPTER ONE

MARY'S STORY AND THE TALE TELEVISION PROMISED

The vision of aging, at least for white, middle-class families, can be viewed through the commercials we frequently see on TV. "A Place for Mom," advertised by TV host and anchorwoman, Joan Lundon, features a trusted, friendly, well-coiffed and tanned star in an upscale dining room warmly advising us that there is a place for mom. The ad shows an inviting, well-appointed space with dining and social amenities. Healthy, well-groomed seniors can live out their lives in a resort-like atmosphere. "Senior Helpers" shows concerned families meeting with young, white caregivers who spend their days in large, nicely decorated homes helping seniors with simple tasks like dressing and meal preparation.

While seniors on the ads may walk with a cane or a walker, they are basically mobile and well-groomed, and they often wear simple, well-put-together outfits with a touch of modern style. Their hair is freshly washed, and the men are neatly shaven.

The residences themselves are modern and spacious. Whether in a senior residence or at home, seniors are shown in rooms free of clutter, with comfortable furniture and vistas of gardens. In a local ad aired in the San Francisco Bay Area, a senior residence in Oakland's Lake Merritt district shows seniors visiting museums, gathering in the dining room overlooking the lake, and relaxing with a cup of tea in a modern apartment. The ad shows a close-up shot of the dining room, where seniors are serenaded by a jazz band while dining by candlelight and enjoying a freshly prepared gourmet meal.

The images are similar to those in marketing brochures for a cruise ship or upscale hotel. This marketing and recruitment effort is the face of a multi-billion-dollar private, for-profit market for senior living facilities that includes a wide spectrum of living options, from independent senior apartments, to assisted living facilities, to skilled nursing homes and residential care homes. The U.S. assisted living facility market size alone was valued at $83.2 billion in 2020.[2]

Sadly, as often is the case, the life presented on TV is not so easily had. The quality can vary greatly between facilities, often differing from the portrait presented in advertising, and the costs any of these facilities can be staggering. Further separating our seniors from the life they're told they can have as they age is the fact that applicable insurance or government subsidies have many restrictions. These costs are largely born by the residents and their families. Availability of a space can be limited and transitioning between types of facilities can be a challenge to navigate. With few exceptions, these institutions have become the de facto standard for middle-class retirees.

What I have come to understand is that the images you see on TV of senior living are really not meant for the middle class at all.

Institutional living, supported by private capital and subsidized by government funding, defines the boundaries of our imagination of how seniors are supposed to live. This skewed portrait has become the standard. In the United State, there is little programmatic support for keeping seniors in their homes and even less support for the caregivers who support them to do so. The private sector caters to wealthy seniors living in resort-like settings. For seniors at the poverty level, Medicaid pays for institutional living in skilled nursing facilities.

In fact, there is a coming crisis for middle income seniors in need of housing and home health assistance in their later years. A recent study concluded that "Unfortunately, these settings are often out of the financial reach of many of this country's eight million middle-income seniors (those ages seventy-five and older). The private seniors housing industry has generally focused on higher-income people instead. We project that by 2029 there will be 14.4 million middle-income seniors, 60 percent of whom will have mobility limitations and 20 percent of whom will have high health care and functional needs. While many of these seniors will likely need the level of care provided in seniors housing, we project that 54 percent of seniors will not have sufficient financial resources to pay for it."[3]

This study, published in Health Affairs in April 2019, could not anticipate the impact of COVID-19, which has only exacerbated an already dire outlook. The dramatic rise in unemployment and the negative impact on retirement savings from a volatile stock market will increase the stress on retirement plans and the investment income seniors rely on.

My mother experienced first-hand the gap between her expectations of her lifestyle in retirement and the reality of running out of money in her nineties. My mother went from having the proverbial $1 million nest egg to living out the end of her life in a trailer park and then in a Medicaid bed in a skilled nursing facility. As her daughter and caregiver, I was responsible for helping her navigate these changes and for identifying options and trade-offs as her care needs exceeded her dwindling budget.

By all accounts from financial advisors on the American aging experience, my mother should have been okay. She was far from it. So, what then of the people who aren't starting from my mother's position of privilege? How bad is the deficit between what they have and what they'll ultimately need in our current system?

MORE THAN A CAUTIONARY TALE

My family's experience is in part a cautionary tale. The reality is that even with sizable savings the image of middle-class retirement is likely out of reach for many families. This came as a surprise to me and to my mother. There are elements of my experience, the solutions we found, and the things we learned that were positive and could be used by other middle-aged family members looking to provide for their parents. There are other aspects of my experience with my mother, Mary, that are meant to raise a red flag as families work to support their aging parents.

My family is white, and we would consider ourselves middle class. While Mary's story included a struggle to rise above the expectations of her immigrant parents, our life as a family in the suburbs of San Francisco was fairly typical of the post-war, middle-class experience. Her fall into poverty was not the culmination of a life-long struggle, as it is for so many. Mary's story highlights the experience that can await the middle class as they age past their earnings and their health needs overtake their income. It was a painful and frightening journey from self-sufficiency and heightened expectations to dependency and the hard reality of facing difficult financial trade-offs. It happened to Mary, and it can happen to your mother or grandmother.

In sharing our story, I want to provide basic information about available programs, their eligibility requirements, and the gaps. Program requirements vary from state to state, and in some case from county to county. Our experience was based in California, where my mother was accessing programs from 2010 to when she passed in 2018. Do to COVID, much in the elder-care landscape has changed since then, sadly I fear for the worse. Please use our experience only as a high-level guide as you seek to explore options and specific eligibility requirements of programs available in your community.

Aging women are a fast-growing demographic facing poverty. My hope is that in sharing my experience with my mother, children of the sandwich generation will be more prepared to help their parents navigate the challenges of aging in America. I also hope that the challenges that my mother faced can be addressed by shoring up the gaps in the social services safety net. COVID-19 has shown us the vulnerability of seniors in care facilities. It has also shown us that families, communities, and government can mobilize to provide health services to those in need as well—there is hope.

COVID-19 has also shown us the supreme vulnerability of the frail elderly living in institutional settings. According to an estimate compiled by the New York Times, one third of all COVID-19 deaths have been at long-term care facilities for older adults, including nursing homes, assisted-living facilities, memory care facilities, retirement and senior communities and rehabilitation facilities.

We need a new model to care for our seniors. What had been a challenge for individual families has been elevated to a national conversation. How can we best care for our seniors?

In this chapter, I will describe the four types of senior living facilities and the differences between independent living, assisted living, board and care, and skilled nursing, as well as living independently with paid caregivers. I have direct experience with all these options. I will describe the services offered, provide cost estimates, and review payment options in light of my family's experiences. The chapter ends by including strategies that helped navigate these options on my mother's behalf and including a recognition that the existing options for seniors are not working now and will not scale to meet the need of the aging Baby Boomer cohort. This will leave many, especially women, to end their lives in institutions and in poverty.

I had many wonderful moments with my mother. And I had many stressful, frustrating, and challenging times. I hope that in sharing my experiences your precious time with your aging parents can include more time for celebration and sharing and less time responding to crisis and navigating bureaucracy.

LEAVING THE FAMILY HOME

My mother chose to enter an independent living facility in her late seventies. She had been living alone in the suburban home in the hills of San Bruno that she moved into as a bride in 1960. It was a split-level tract home with three bedrooms upstairs; the kitchen, dining, and living room at the entry level; and a basement recreation room downstairs at the garage level. The back yard was also a split level, with the upper half dominated by pine trees and some aged vegetable and flower gardens, and the lower level covered in cement. The neighborhood was a mixture of blue- and white-collar workers and their families. A single policeman lived on one side and a Lutheran minister and his family on the other. Other neighbors included an insurance agent and a machinist. As was typical in the 1960s, few of the women worked outside of the home. My mother was an exception.

The topography was rugged. Although the houses were lined up next to each other, our street had a steep pitch. Getting to a grocery store on foot required a walk down a steep hill to the end of the block and then an even steeper climb to the top of another hill. I did it a lot as a young child, and it left me winded by the time I crested Claremont Drive to arrive at the Five and Dime. In addition, San Bruno is not Laguna Beach. The weather in the hills was frequently cold and windy. Even in the summer, you would have to wear a sweater or jacket. For my mother, walking to the store was out of the question. She had to drive to get to any services. Her church was three miles away in the older part of San Bruno.

By 2000, the house had gotten too much for my mother to manage on her own. Although my brother had lived at home into his thirties, he had moved on with his life, and my mother was on her own in the large house. She had a gardener, so the yard was maintained, but she could not stand to have someone come in to clean or assist with cooking. While increased levels of assistance may have kept my mother in the family home longer, she was reluctant to have someone come into her space on a regular basis. The few attempts at hiring a housecleaner ended in frustration as my mother always felt that she could do a better job and was wasting her money.

The challenge of getting groceries presented another obstacle. Today, there are many delivery services, but twenty years ago these business models were not in place. My mother never learned how to operate a computer or a smart phone. The tools and services available on the internet were not part of her world. The "Greatest Generation" may be last cohort to live such a reality.

Feeling a bit lonely and isolated, my mother started to look at options for where she wanted to live out her retirement. It was not an easy decision to sell the house. The family had many memories there, and the logistics of cleaning out almost fifty years of accumulated furniture, knickknacks, and papers were overwhelming. She went back and forth with the decision until she fell down the stairs carrying laundry to the washing machine in the garage. Fortunately, she did not break a bone or worse, but the fall left her shaken.

The real estate market in San Bruno was also heating up. When I was growing up, San Bruno was very much an industrial suburb with the United Airlines maintenance hub being the largest employer. There were many machine shops and other small manufacturing concerns serving the airport and San Francisco. By 2000, like much of the San Francisco Bay Area, high tech started to dominate the labor market. The old site of the Veteran's Administration office was transformed into the headquarters for Gap. Now YouTube is one of the city's largest employers. San Bruno has come a long way, and so have housing prices.

My parents purchased the house in 1960 for less than $20,000. When she sold the house, it was worth almost half a million dollars. Today, the house would sell for over a million! My mother was confident that the nest egg she had accumulated from the sale of the home, the sale of her accounting practice, and the money inherited from her parents would allow her to live comfortably in retirement. All totaled, she had amassed that magic number that financial analysts and wealth-management advisors hold out as the holy grail for retirees—$1 million. I am sure it felt like a small fortune.

My mother started looking at housing options. Should she sell the house and buy a small condo closer to transportation and shopping? That was an option. However, when she added up the condo HOA fees and looked at options in the fast-appreciating real estate market, she was not convinced that this was the right option for her.

She had friends who were moving into independent living facilities. Visiting them she appreciated the amenities and services they provided. She started looking at the many options available on the San Francisco Peninsula, which had had a full range of senior Independent Living options from the lavish to the modest. The facility that my mother chose was on the lower end of price range and located on a major thoroughfare close to shopping. A hospital and medical center were less than a mile away. It seemed like a practical choice at the time. Busy raising my teens, I knew little about senior housing. I learned a lot over time.

INDEPENDENT LIVING APARTMENT

Independent living apartments are just that—apartments designed for independent living. Seniors looking to live in independent living apartments must meet a threshold for mobility and cognition documented by a physician. While there is some latitude, the layout and service level does not support seniors whose physical and psychological needs require on-going medical or nursing assistance.

Apartments can range from small studios to large one- and two-bedroom units. The units come unfurnished, allowing the senior to bring their own furniture and décor. Both of the independent living apartments Mary lived in had one bedroom with ample storage, and a balcony large enough for a chair and plants. The units were carpeted in the living room and bedroom, with tile or linoleum in the kitchen. Apartments come with bathrooms, which may have some special features for seniors, such as grips and bars and an emergency call button. Kitchens are standard with storage, a stove, and microwave. Some come with dishwashers. The location, square footage of the unit, and amenities offered govern the price.

Independent living facilities do not track or limit a resident's whereabouts. Mary was free to go. The doors were locked at 10 pm, but she had a key, and there was a buzzer and an attendant in the case she was locked out after hours. Front-desk staff would provide a welfare check if requested, but my mother was free to spend days in her apartment or to leave for trips with her family without any restrictions. There was on-site maintenance, which provide routine repairs and keep the common areas clean. Unlike a regular apartment complex where neighbors may encounter each other only at the mailbox or pool, independent living apartments have more shared services designed to support seniors living independently and communally.

Both independent living apartment complexes Mary lived in had a coin-operated laundry room, a library, an activities room, and a dining room. Both offered transportation with a regular route to the mall, local senior centers, drug stores, and grocery stores. By appointment, my mother could also use the bus or car transport to get to doctor appointments. Both centers also had secure parking—when Mary first moved into her first apartment, she was still driving, and she paid extra to secure her car in the garage. The apartment complexes also had an on-site hair salon offering a full range of services at market rate. Weekly housekeeping services (cleaning the bathroom and kitchen, vacuuming, and light dusting) were also included, though personal laundry or daily dishes was not.

Cable services, telephone landlines, and electricity costs were not included in the cost of the apartment—just like any other apartment. Some facilities offer free wi-fi. Residents need to have independent contracts with the local service providers. Heating and cooling costs can be quite significant. In the first facility in San Mateo, heating and cooling costs were moderate since the climate was temperate. Mary's apartment did not have direct sunlight since it faced the courtyard; it was not too hot or too dark. In Placerville, which is in the mountains, my mother's heating and cooling bill was significant since the climate is more extreme with temperatures over 100 degrees in the summer and snow in the winter.

For Mary, the best feature of independent living apartments was the social activity calendar. Activities included exercise classes, crafts, games, movies, and religious services. The facilities had an Activity Director who created a calendar that had at least one activity per day. Birthdays and holidays were celebrated with seasonal decorations and festivities. One of the two facilities had a happy hour every Friday with wine, appetizers, and a piano bar!

The dining room offered three meals a day—breakfast, lunch, and dinner. The dining room was not like a college cafeteria, but more like a fancy, if dated, restaurant. There was a host who assisted the residents with finding an open seat at table and made sure they were safely seated, securing their walker. The dining room was much like a cruise ship with coveted tables and some jockeying between groups to get a seat at what was perceived to be the "popular table." Wait staff presented the dining options and served the meal.

Like a college meal plan, my mother could choose how many meals she wanted to eat in the dining room since she also had a kitchen in her apartment. Mary never ate breakfast in the dining room, preferring to get up later and have breakfast in her apartment. She always ate dinner in the dining room and purchased a meal plan with a limited number of lunches per month. When she did not feel well, both facilities offered the option of bringing a meal to her room. There were a limited number of free deliveries, and then the facility added on a per meal charge for deliveries.

The food at both facilities was good. It's hard to please dozens of seniors with many dietary restrictions. The chefs strived to create a diverse menu, but my mother always found the food to be very bland and took every opportunity she could get to lobby the chef for her favorite—Italian food. On pasta night, Mary always got a second helping. While my mother was an insulin-dependent diabetic, the kitchen staff did not restrict her diet. In independent living, adhering to dietary restrictions is the responsibility of the senior. If Mary chose to have dessert or even a second dessert, no one was going to stop her.

While both facilities had an on-site nurse, the expectation was that the seniors living in independent living were independent. Seniors were expected to take care of their own physical and medical needs. In both facilities where my mother lived, there was a large cadre of home health aides who were independent contractors available for hire by the hour. As my mother aged, her mobility decreased and her ability to manage her diabetes and the complications arising from this chronic condition increased. She made increasing use of these private-hire, home-health aides.

At $20 or more per hour, payment for the aides was a significant expense. At one facility, the minimum visit would be one half-hour. At the other facility, the aides would charge for a fifteen-minute visit, which provided the flexibility my mother needed as she aged. The aide could come for half an hour to an hour in the morning to measure my mother's blood sugar and assist in her insulin injection, fix breakfast, and help my mother get dressed. They would pop in for a quick check at lunch and then for her nighttime injection. They also helped with laundry and daily cleaning.

The quality of the home health aides varied. The facility didn't employee these workers directly, nor was the facility responsible for ensuring they were properly licensed. Since my mother was an insulin-dependent diabetic, it was a violation of the licensing requirements for home health aides to perform an injection. The aide could measure the insulin and perform the draw but would need to hand it to my mother to inject herself. Newer, pre-loaded insulin pens made this easier. However, as my mother became less able and her vision and dexterity declined, all of the aides actually assisted my mother with her injections.

Independent living facilities are not cheap. For some months, depending on the level of private care, my mother was spending between $6,000 and $7,000! This did not include any discretionary spending like trips and gifts. This level of spending was hard to maintain since my mother's monthly income from Social Security was $1,700. Payment for all costs above that came from her principal and any investment income that she saved over the course of a lifetime of work. This is all a private-pay expense as independent living facilities do not take Medicare or Medicaid. My mother did not have long-term care insurance, but such polices can pay for a limited number of caregiver hours for the period of time specified in the policy. Medical expenses can be tax deductible after a certain limit as well, so there is some hope to get a modest tax refund or at least a tax credit.

Below is a sample monthly budget based on my experience with my mother.

Rent	$4,500
Caregiver 30 days x 2 hours per day x $20/hr	$1,200
Utilities	$200
Food (in addition to meals provided)	$400
Medical Insurance	$75
Medication and Diapers	$250
Other—Hair Salon. Clothes, etc.	$100
Total	**$6,725**

Depending on the location, independent living costs can far exceed my above estimate and easily out-pace a middle-class senior's retirement savings. Some facilities require an upfront deposit, which can be many thousands of dollars, in addition to the monthly fee.

HINDSIGHT IS ALWAYS 20/20

As a best practice, I would encourage adult children to engage their parents in a serious discussion about budgeting to understand if their plan passes the sniff test of reasonableness. I was not able to have this discussion with my mother. Her credentialing as a CPA precluded her taking advice from her children. I don't think my mother was unique in this regard.

If I was to do it all over again, I would have pressed to make sure that my mother was receiving counsel from a trusted advisor. It did not have to be me, but perhaps my uncle or a professional colleague could have helped.

The challenge with budgeting for any retiree is that it is impossible to know the denominator. Mary had no idea that she would live to 94, although her own mother had lived to 95. Financial advisors opine that retirees should budget to withdraw no more than 4 percent per year from their principle and investment income in order to be prudent. Looking back, my mother's budget was 5 percent of her total assets and income each year. She was spending over $70,000 per year on independent living with an income from Social Security of approximately $20,000. All told, $50,000 per year from a nest egg of $1,000,000 is roughly a 5 percent burn rate.

With fewer than 13 percent of seniors able to rely on a pension for a guaranteed income, seniors need to be able to successfully navigate the complex banking and investment industry to manage their savings and portfolio of investments in order to generate income for life. That is for those seniors who have savings. According to a PwC report, one in four Americans have no retirement savings and many more have saved much less than what they will need.[4] The stock market crash of 2009 and the subsequent low interest rates resulted in a significant loss of both principle and income for many seniors. As we enter the post COVID-era, inflation may also play a factor in reducing buying power for those on a fixed income. Incredibly, over a thirty-year period, 3.9 percent inflation brings the purchasing power of $100 to $32, and the latest Consumer Price index report shows inflation rate as of March 2022 is more than 8 percent.[5]

My mother's initial budget was high, but that was not the biggest issue. Her failure to actually stick to her budget and to adjust accordingly was the insurmountable challenge. Escalating expenses should have necessitated a significant re-budgeting exercise and an immediate change of lifestyle. Admittedly, that would have been difficult when my mother still had a healthy bank balance but saving money in her late seventies and early eighties would have provided her with a longer runway and more options.

But institutional living had captured my mother's imagination (as it does for many) and since she could initially afford to live in an independent living apartment, it was difficult for her to see that there was a problem with her plan, or that such a living arrangement might be finite, timewise. In fact, my mother firmly believed that she was doing the right thing for herself and for her family. Her perspective was that this was how seniors were supposed to live, a perspective reinforced daily by American marketing and advertising around the elder-care industry. She felt that the services provided by the facility would unburden her family from the responsibility for her care.

THE TRANSITION TO ASSISTED LIVING

After twelve years at an Independent Living facility, my mother slipped in the bathroom and suffered a multiple compound fracture. Following surgery and a three-month stint in a rehabilitation facility, my mother needed to go to an assisted living facility since she was rehabbing slowly and was still in a wheelchair. Independent living precludes individuals from living in apartments who they deem not medically able to do so. The regulations vary, but all independent living facilities require a medical evaluation and can turn away seniors who they deem to be not medically able to live independently. My mother was not able to return to her independent living apartment after her fall.

It can get very contentious when a resident's health, cognition, and mobility decline to the point where the independent living facility deems it necessary that the senior can no longer continue to live independently and requires a higher level of care. Activities of daily living (ADLs) are routine activities people do every day without assistance. There are six basic ADLs: eating, bathing, getting dressed, toileting, transferring, and continence.

The fall, the ninety days in rehab, and the transition to assisted living marked a significant turning point for my mother. In her time in independent living, my mother was hospitalized for urinary tract infections and fell off the exercise equipment, breaking her collar bone. But she was able to rehab from those illnesses and injuries and continue to live independently. That was no longer the case by 2012

Assisted living facilities provide a higher level of support than independent living apartments. Some facilities have both types of care types in a single facility, independent and assisted living. Both of the independent living facilities my mother lived in had a separate wing for assisted living. However, when my mother's needs changed, neither facility had an opening, and my mother had to move. It is not a given that when a patient's needs change that there will be an opening in their current facility.

Assisted living provides daily supervised medical care, medication management, the opportunity for rehabilitation, and medically managed diets. There are less opportunities for social activities. At the facility where my mother lived, many of the patients had mobility issues and most had memory issues or were in the beginning stages of Alzheimer's. Memory care facilities are assisted living facilities that focus on the care of patients with dementia. Many of these also have the option for skilled nursing care.

The cost for a small single room in the assisted living facility exceeded $6,000 per month for my mother. Aside from some limited demonstration projects, Medicare does not pay for assisted living. Payment options include private pay and long-term care insurance, which is limited per the specifics of the policy. There is also a program through the Veteran's Administration that covers some costs for veterans, although neither of my parents served in the armed forces. In some states, there may be assisted living facilities that accept Medicaid, but in Northern California there were only a handful of demonstration project slots, and these had a long waiting list. My mother paid out of pocket for assisted living, though the cost was actually slightly less than independent living since assistance with daily living activities, medication management, and all meals were included.

Still, the transition was hard for my mother. She had to move from a spacious, one-bedroom apartment to a small single room studio to make the economics work within her budget. The assisted living facility was the right decision and the only option to get my mother fully rehabbed and able to walk again. In addition, the medication management and dietary monitoring did wonders to get my mother's diabetes under control.

However, my mother chafed under the regimentation, physical rehab, medication management, and dietary restrictions. In addition, her social life was reduced since most of the residents weren't conversant. I received multiple calls from the assisted living administration about my mother's lack of adherence to the rules, and ultimately when frustrations met a boiling point, she lashed out at the staff.

My role as my mother's caregiver changed with the shift as well. When my mother was living independently, I lived about twenty miles away. I would visit about twice a month and take her to medical appointments when she would ask. Most of the time, she took the transport from the facility. As she grew older, I would take her grocery shopping and to the drugstore since it became increasingly hard for her to manage her groceries and to get on and off the bus. I can recall numerous arguments in the grocery store about my mother's choices to purchase cookies and ice cream and a Snicker's bar at the check-out stand. I remember attending doctor's visits with my mother where her internal medicine practitioner vented his frustration with my mother's noncompliance with her insulin regime. He regaled my mother about the ravages of diabetes—kidney failure, heart disease, loss of limbs, blindness. My mother just looked at him and shrugged, saying, "You have to die of something."

At this point, my mother was very vigorous in defending her independence and affirming her rights to make all decisions regarding her healthcare and finances. My mother was in her mid-eighties, and I was in my early fifties with two children living at home in high school. As a mother of teenagers, I was used to negotiating the tricky balance between supporting autonomy and laying down clear boundaries to make sure that no one got hurt. As a parent, I tended to err on the side of freedom, but with my mother, I could not understand or support her decision-making process. It appeared to be ill-advised and willfully self-destructive. Teens could take risks or be uniformed, but my mother's stubborn willfulness made two teens look like wise owls by comparison. In twelve years of school per child, I had two calls to the office. With my mother at assisted living, the calls came monthly. She struck a worker. She made unkind statements to staff and other residents. She struck a resident. She was non-compliant. Eventually the call came. She had to go.

Fortunately, despite her protestations, she had received good care and was now able to walk, albeit with a walker. My mother had called and made the arrangements to transition back to her independent living apartment. She squeaked by the physical and returned to an independent apartment over my best judgement and advice. The one concession I was able to negotiate was that she could not shower alone. She needed to have supervised bathing assistance to avoid another serious fall.

I will leave my mother back at her independent living apartment for the time being. She has her feet up in her recliner and is reading Reader's Digest with a cup of instant coffee and a cookie. For a white, middle-class professional, her experience has been almost like the ads. She went to the dining room, clapped and sang along with the bands, took the bus to events, and made friends. Yes, she had injuries and hospitalizations and was depleting her nest egg at a fast clip, but she was living the life. We will pick up Mary's story with the discussion of rehabilitation and skilled nursing facilities, but first let's take a deeper look at how residential care homes work.

RESIDENTIAL CARE HOME

A third type of senior facility is a residential care home, or board and care. Both my father and my maternal grandmother lived in board and care facilities at the end of their lives. Since my father died early, my experience with residential care home facilities dates back to the 1980s. At that time, residential care homes were much cheaper than assisted living facilities. When I last researched this option for my mother, they continued to be cheaper, but still cost upwards of $3,500 per month in the Placerville area. A co-worker confided that she was paying in excess of $6,000 per month for a board and care room for her mother in the San Francisco Bay area.

Residential care homes are homes in residential neighborhoods where small groups of seniors live with twenty-four-hour care provided by non-nursing staff. They differ from skilled nursing facilities or nursing homes, where skilled nursing staff on are on-site for twenty-four hours per day. Residential care homes offer seniors a room or shared room, three meals a day, and help with managing the activities for daily living. Some offer recreational activities, but in most board and care homes, the focus is on the care of the residents. Since the setting is residential, board and care homes can feel more like a home. In some, like the one my grandmother lived in, residents are able to bring their own furniture. My father's room came furnished. With the small number of patients, care can be individualized. However, for extroverted seniors like my mother, the small number of people to interact with can be boring or limiting.

My father resided in a board and care following cancer surgery. He had extensive medical needs and cycled between the hospital, skilled nursing or rehab facilities, and the board and care. My maternal grandmother lived in a larger board and care where they had a limited set of activities. She was not mobile and needed the round-the-clock care that a board and care could provide. Residential care homes are not licensed to care for patients who need skilled nursing care. For example, residential care homes are not licensed for patients with feeding tubes. Diabetic care is a tricky one. Once again, I was told that my mother would have to be able to inject herself.

REHABILITATION AND SKILLED NURSING

A fourth care option for seniors is a skilled nursing facility— a nursing home. This is what we all dread—the possibility that our loved one may need the level of care that only a skilled nursing facility can provide. Skilled nursing facilities exist to provide twenty-four-hour skilled nursing care for patients. Many skilled nursing facilities also offer rehabilitation services. Sometimes the patients receiving rehab are in the same facility, sometimes they are in a separate wing or set of rooms. My mother's first encounter with a skilled nursing facility was for a period of rehab following her collar bone break.

It's important to note that Medicare will pay for rehabilitation, but it will not pay for long-term care. The Medicare guidelines for payment for rehabilitation are as follows:

> "After you have been in a hospital for at least three days, Medicare will pay for inpatient rehab for up to 100 days in a benefit period. A benefit period starts when you go into the hospital. It ends when you have not received any hospital care or skilled nursing care for 60 days. Medicare pays for the first 20 days at 100%. For the next 80 days, you must pay a daily co-payment. Medicare does not pay for rehab after 100 days. If you go into the hospital for at least 3 days after one benefit period has ended, a new benefit period starts. You can have as many benefit periods as you need.[6]

While Medicare does not pay for long-term skilled nursing care, Medicaid does. States may have unique requirements. You can find more detailed information about state-specific Medicaid eligibility requirements on Medicaid.gov. Generally, an individual must be income eligible to qualify for this support. An individual can have no more than $2,000 in countable liquid assets when they apply. Generally, the individual's home and car are exempted from being considered since they are not liquid and in many cases the individual may return to the home. Upon entry into skilled nursing, the individual surrender's their Social Security check to the institution. My mother was allowed to retain $20 per month for her personal expenses.

My mother did not own a home or a car when she entered skilled nursing. If she did, she could still be eligible for Medicaid, but federal law requires that states put a lien on a recipient's home and can demand repayment for services once the recipient passes. There are exceptions to this, especially if a spouse or dependent child is living in the home. However, the government is keen on recouping costs if there is an asset which can be liquidated from the estate.

There may be some recognition that the "spend down" requirement has resulted in driving seniors into poverty. The State of California recently passed a law that beginning July, 2022, the asset limit for seniors to receive Medicaid support for long term care needs to be raised. The plan is to incrementally raise the limit over the next few years from the current restriction of $2,000 to as high as $130,000 for single individuals and $267,000 for a couple. The state will also increase the focus on estate recovery. So, although, the spend down rule will be removed up front, the state will recoup the cost of care from the estate.

My mother had a very positive experience in the two facilities where she received rehabilitation services covered under Medicare and her supplemental private insurance policy. The first facility was attached to a hospital on the San Francisco Bay Peninsula and the second was in Placerville. Rehabilitation facilities and the services they provide cater to a wide set of patients. In addition to seniors, there are people of all ages rehabilitating from accidents, surgery, or illness. Skilled and credentialled occupational and physical therapists create plans for the patient with measurable goals. Patients need to make progress to stay in the rehabilitation program.

The patient rooms in the skilled nursing facility where my mother received rehabilitation services and ultimately resided as a long- term care patient were very hospital-like in nature. Rooms were shared. My mother was in double and once in a triple room. She had a hospital bed, a small nightstand, and a small locker-like closet. The only concession to privacy was a curtain that could be drawn around the bed for changing or bathing. Bathrooms were shared as well. In the Placerville center, the room did not even have space for a chair for visitors. There was one TV in the room, and negotiations over the programming were a frequent source of conflict. In both facilities, my mother was fortunate to have a bed by a window with a garden or courtyard view.

One of the biggest challenges in a skilled nursing facility is the lack of privacy and control over one's person and possessions. The routine is highly regimented. Just like a hospital, nursing home residents can be woken up for medication or for routine care like bathing, toothbrushing, or for meals. In a shared room my mother frequently complained that her roommate would call out in the night or would mistakenly turn on the light or TV. Sometimes it was hard to get a good night's sleep.

Keeping track of clothing is a huge challenge, too. All clothing items need to be clearly marked with the patient's name in permanent marker. That being said, it's important not to bring any fancy clothes to a skilled nursing facility. Everyone tries their best, but with dozens of patient's clothes in the same laundry facility, things get mixed up. I frequently found my mother's roommate wearing her clothes and my mother wearing some unidentified item of clothing. As they say, it all comes out in the wash. But I know this can be a source of frustration for nursing home residents and their families.

Personal items are also at risk for getting lost or broken. My mother would not part with her purse. We removed anything of value and personal identification from her wallet, but she slept with her purse in her bed, nonetheless. The most challenging nursing home experience with lost possessions was not with my mother, but with my father. My father had lost his larynx to cancer before he died and used a mechanical voice box to speak. In one rehabilitation facility where he was a patient following surgery, his voice box went missing along with all his underwear! He was not a happy camper when they discharged him wearing a diaper. Fortunately, his voice box was returned when it was realized that it had no value.

Despite the lack of privacy and control over one's person, skilled nursing facilities and the staff that work in them provide an invaluable service to our most vulnerable frail elderly patients. At the point in her life where my mother needed twenty-four-hour care and assistance in all daily living activities, we were both extremely grateful to have a bed in a highly rated skilled nursing facility. Caring professionals helped her to do everything from sitting up and getting cleaned up to transferring to the wheelchair for a ride to the dining room. The energetic activities director did his best to provide programming for patients with varying levels of cognitive and physical abilities.

Entering a skilled nursing facility, you will probably encounter a line of elderly patients in wheelchairs lining the hallway, waiting. A large portion of the day is spent waiting: waiting for meals, waiting for medication, waiting for an activity to start, waiting to re-enter the room or even the facility. Skilled nursing facilities have ample security and patients are not allowed to freely leave. When I took my mother out from the skilled nursing facility, I needed to sign her out and sign her back in.

COVID-19 has shed a spotlight on the risks to patients living in skilled nursing facilities. When my mother was a resident, an outbreak of the flu spread throughout the Placerville facility. Staff and visitors wore masks and hand sanitizers were spread throughout the facility. The skilled nursing staff had their hands full with most of the residents experiencing vomiting and diarrhea. It is very difficult to keep viruses from spreading in an environment where intimate personal care is required, and patients live in close proximity.

Skilled nursing facilities have been an important part of the care spectrum. By the time my mother entered skilled nursing, it was a matter of life or death. My mother was no longer mobile. She had suffered multiple falls and hospitalizations in a two-week period. She was on hospice and needed round-the-clock care.

THE CYCLE

My mother lived independently in independent living, rehabilitation, assisted living, and skilled nursing. While this sequence represents the spectrum of care from light assistance to round-the-clock attention, the transitions were anything but orderly. Transitions were precipitated by a health crisis or a financial crisis. I was always in reactive mode. I found this to be one of the most difficult aspects of caring for a dependent senior, as I spent years reacting to changing circumstances. The call at work, the scramble to cover my responsibilities, the three-hour drive to the hospital— it became a very familiar pattern, one too many American families know too well.

My mother managed the first transition from living at home to her independent living apartment in San Mateo herself. She was able to clear out the family home, put it on the market, and move in. She was in her late 70s and had many contacts in the community, which was where she had had her accounting practice. Movers, estate agents, and real estate agents all relied on my mother to do their taxes and were happy to help her with this life-changing move. I was fortunate. For many, the cleaning and sale of a family home is an overwhelming challenge.

While in independent living, I helped my mother with shopping and routine trips to the doctor. And I became her authorized Power of Attorney for healthcare when she was hospitalized for complications stemming from her diabetes and her broken collar bone. Fortunately, at this time I lived close by, and the hospital and rehabilitation facilities were close to my mother's home. I could easily collect her mail, bring it to the rehab facility, and check in with the nursing staff. As my mother aged, she relied on me more and more for trips to the grocery store and healthcare providers.

The first emergency transition came following my mother's fall in the bathroom. She experienced a multiple compound fracture requiring surgery and the implant of at steel plate and screws in her left ankle. During recovery, she had a heart attack. My mother was not ready to return to her independent living facility and spent ninety days in a rehabilitation center. The challenge came at the end of the Medicare limit for rehabilitation. My mother was still wheelchair bound then. While she insisted that she was ready and able to return to independent living, the facility deemed that she did not meet the minimum requirement to live independently. Like it or not, my mother would need to go to assisted living.

Discharge is always hard. It would have been a lot more comfortable if we'd had weeks to plan, review different options, and choose the best fit. I have been through at least a dozen discharge scenarios, and it never happens that way. First, it's difficult to pinpoint a discharge date. Whether from a hospital or from a rehabilitation center, discharge timing is not an exact science. It depends on the patient's progress and the availability of an empty bed at the intake facility. Insurance and Medicare/Medicaid also play a role. Healthcare professionals may want a patient to stay a bit longer to realize health gains, but insurers push back and steer towards discharge to free up beds. Social workers try to mediate this push and pull and to provide families with options in a timely manner, but it doesn't always work out that way. "Surprise, we are discharging your parent today!" is a common call for families to receive.

Following the above-mentioned conflict with the assisted living staff and administration, my mother drove the transition back to independent living. I was not onboard with this decision. However, after multiple hard conversations with my mother and the administrator at the assisted living facility, I knew I couldn't change her mind. My mother was competent to make her own decisions still., even though I feared the result could be a poor health outcome.

The next transition was driven by financial considerations. My mother started in 2000 with a nest egg of $1 million. By January 2015, she had less than $100,000 left. She was 90 years old. At her current run rate at the independent living facility in the San Francisco Bay Area, she would be out of money by the end of the year. While my mother had deferred making decisions, she could no longer put it off. I started exploring options.

Living with me was not a realistic option since my partner and I had four college-age children who cycled in and out of our home. Space was already at a premium. More importantly, my mother would not agree to it. She highly valued her independence and believed that the TV lifestyle of the resort-like independent living apartments was what she deserved. Options in the San Francisco Bay Area were all within the same price band. To get the same kind of quality in an independent living facility that she could afford, we would need to look farther away…a lot farther. I was familiar with the foothill community of Placerville and found a facility there with an opening and amenities on par with what my mother had enjoyed in the Bay Area—at half of the price for lodging and food, no less. Caregiving assistance would be an incremental expense.

During Super Bowl weekend, we loaded up my mother and her belongings for the three-hour ride to Placerville. Of course, not everything goes to plan. Somehow my mother's bedframe didn't make it on to the truck. She had her mattress and box spring so she was able to sleep, but since the bed was so low to the ground, she couldn't get out of bed in the morning! Furniture store options were limited in the small mountain town, especially during Super Bowl Sunday. I found a bedframe, but it was too short for her mattress. With a quick trip to Walmart, we scored two small stools, a roll of duct tape, and a C clamp, cobbling together a viable temporary bedframe. This solution became a metaphor for what was to come. We would need to get very creative!

One year later, by January 2016, we had to make another plan. My mother's care needs had escalated, blowing the original budget. She had less than $20,000 in savings now, and the Placerville independent living facility had no options for residents who couldn't pay. She would be out on the street! I had to find shelter for my mother. I found the rare assisted living facility that would accept Medicaid, but it was back in the San Francisco Bay Area. The facility would take my mother as a private pay patient until her resources were exhausted and then would the supplement her ability to pay by qualifying her for Medicaid. There are only a handful of these facilities in Northern California. My mother refused to participate in the intake process. She was reluctant to face another big move and had bonded with her amazing caregiver. Ironically, after months of complaining about moving to the sticks, my mother did not want to move back to the city.

THE LITTLE TRAILER

What to do? I had to find a very low-cost home for my mother. Her Social Security check would be used for her medical and care needs. The waiting list for Senior Housing was three years! That was not an immediate option. I explored board and care homes, but at $3,000 per month or more, I would need to supplement my mother's income by more than $2,000 per month. I couldn't do this without jeopardizing my children's college education. The sandwich had become a vice. I was caught between paying for my mother or paying for my children.

It sounded crazy at the time, but I purchased a single-wide trailer in a Senior Mobile Home Park in Placerville. I had to invest $12,000 to purchase the trailer. While this came out of pocket, I knew that when my mother passed, I could sell it and recoup the investment, so I was willing to take out a loan.

The trailer was in rough shape. The previous owner was a single man who had not made any improvements since its original purchase in the 1980s. Wall-to-wall shag carpet! Fortunately, I had been training for just this opportunity for years. I am an avid HGTV fan and watch all of those TV shows where they take fixer uppers and transform them into gems. If Chip and Joanna could do it, so could I. I had six weeks to transform this humble abode into a safe and clean space for my mother. I found a wonderful contractor who was also very creative. We replaced the carpet with laminate, painted the paneling a fresh white, reconfigured a closet to add a washer/dryer, and replaced the entire kitchen. We sourced an oak cabinet set on craigslist for $400. I invested another $12,000 in the trailer, and it was just about ready when my mother moved in March 2016.

The eleven-by-twenty foot, single-wide mobile home had a large bedroom where my mother was able to have her twin bed, dresser, and large bookcase filled with family photos and her collection of teacups and collectables from over 70 years honoring the British royal family. I purchased a low-pile rug, which helped keep the floor warm without creating a tripping hazard. There was a large closet that easily accommodated all of my mother's clothes and built-in shelving that we used to store additional bedding and towels and her hamper.

The bathroom was very sizable with a shower over the tub. I had an emergency button installed for safety, which activated the same service as her wearable call button. I updated the medicine cabinet removing the old rusty one and freshened everything with a coat of paint and new drawer pulls on the vanity.

The living room and kitchen was combined and the heart of the home. Visitors walked into this space from the slider off the large deck. The U-shaped kitchen cabinetry had a light finish with dark gray countertops. I pulled out the gas stove since it presented a potential fire hazard. In its place I put a cheerful yellow appliance caddy with a microwave and electric burner. These appliances, along with a crock pot, a toaster oven, and coffee pot were sufficient to cook simple meals.

Next to the kitchen, there was a small table with a folding leaf and two chairs where my mother used to eat her breakfast and visit with her caregiver over meals. The living room had space for a desk, two large comfortable chairs, and the TV cabinet housing my mother's collection of photo albums. There was even room for her large oak curio cabinet with her collection of Hummels and ceramics collected from years of global travel. There was ample space for my mother to navigate the space of the trailer using her walker.

Living in the trailer allowed my mother's entire Social Security check to be directed to her healthcare—payments to caregivers, medical visit co-pays, medication co-pays, insurance, and diapers. There was still a gap—food, utilities, and the space rent. I worked to enroll my mother in as many programs as I could find to support low-income seniors—SNAP (food stamps), Meals on Wheels, HEAP (heating assistance), LifeLine (telephone). However, there was always a monthly budget gap, between $500–$1,000 per month, which I filled.

My mother lived in her little trailer until November of 2017, when multiple falls in a week and her growing disorientation precipitated a hospital stay. Upon discharge, she lacked the mobility to return home, so she went to rehabilitation. After the ninety-day period, she remained unable to walk and continued to reside at the skilled nursing facility, receiving hospice services until her passing in August of 2018.

AGING IN AMERICA

The United States and our capitalistic economic system is singularly fearful that government-funded support for basic needs robs the individual of an incentive to work. It wasn't long ago that the only option for the elderly was to work until they dropped dead or rely solely on the support of their children. Government programs are still looked upon with suspicion, even for a group that is deemed worthy of help like the dependent elderly.

As this chapter has shown us, the safety net for the elderly is precarious at best. A middle-class, college-educated business owner like my mother can end her life in poverty. While this chapter shows how my mother and I adjusted to her changing situation, the answer for the millions of us in this situation cannot continue to be a singularly resourceful response to crisis. Now is the time to advocate for a comprehensive policy overhaul.

The United States is the only developed county without a comprehensive plan for the payment and delivery of medical care. The defacto standard for care is now institutional living. With the exception of Medicare reimbursement for ninety days in rehabilitation and Medicaid's payment for the impoverished to reside in skilled nursing, there are few alternatives to individual and family payment.

As we've seen, senior housing and medical care is big business in the United State. Our capitalistic system seeks to monetize those who cannot actively contribute to the economy through their labor. Historically, the pendulum has swung between institutionalization and in-home care; but at this time, institutional living has captured our seniors.

Ultimately, my mother's story is one of hope. Feisty to the last, she was mourned by her family, her caregivers, members of her church community, and even her clients from years past. I was able to help my mother build and rely on a small community of care in the senior trailer park. Resident home health aides, the Catholic church, county programs, and a volunteer led food bank and lending library patched together a caring network of support for my housebound, indigent mother. There are many stories of communities pulling together to create a safe and supportive place for seniors. Later chapters in this book will discuss options for community based care in hopes of demonstrating that there is a path towards a better balance of eldercare—one where seniors are supported, autonomous, surrounded by community, and where daughters and wives do not have to bear the undue brunt of caretaking responsibilities.

In the next chapter, we will explore how this system came to be and how generations before us fought to ensure that the elderly (and especially the impoverished elderly) could receive healthcare, housing, and income.

CHAPTER TWO

CARING FOR OUR ANCESTORS

We live in a time where the drawbacks of institutional living have been further highlighted by COVID-19. The global pandemic essentially imprisoned seniors living in care facilities and the death rate rose to levels of outrageous loss. This grim reality may push us to create innovative solutions to create and support home and community-based care that enables seniors to continue to contribute to their home communities, while caring for others and being cared for themselves. However, our history has shown us that the best solutions for seniors, the disabled, and the poor are not always the solutions society is willing to provide. This chapter looks at the story of how we have cared for our seniors from Colonial America to the present.

In the United States, there is a history of institutionalizing the poor, elderly, and infirm. There have also been instances where societal pressures prompted public payments of cash or in-kind support to enable individuals in need of assistance to stay in their homes. The United States experiences an ongoing conflict between the moral imperative to care for those who are not able to care for themselves and the fear of creating a moral hazard for those deemed to "lazy" to work or fend for themselves. By making high standards of care available through the government as a human right and programmatic entitlement, the concern is that personal and familial responsibility would diminish—why take care of things yourself if a safety net exists to do it for you? Sadly, this flawed logic persists today in our country.

In our capitalist system, if you are not generating wealth through your labor, your body can be monetized to make money for someone else. In his book, *The Poorhouse: America's Forgotten Institution*, author and professor David Wagner explores the fraught history in depth: From colonial times when the dependent elderly were actually auctioned off to the lowest bid for board and care to today's overpriced institutional housing options—somebody is getting rich.[7]

Any discussion about eldercare in the United States must take race and class into account. These distinctions underpin the development of our nation's healthcare systems, resulting in costly and ineffective care for all of us and vastly different options and outcomes for seniors of color and the working class.

But why has institutional living become the standard? Certainly not because it's in the best interest of seniors. The culprit, like many things, is profitability. In our capitalist system, if you are not generating wealth through your labor, your body can be monetized to make money for someone else. Investors in senior housing facilities, including private equity firms and the monied investors in Real Estate Investment Trusts (REITs), make out very well in current-day America, even if many of our seniors do not. The private sector caters to wealthy seniors living in resort-like, institutional settings. For seniors at the poverty level, Medicaid pays for institutional living in skilled nursing facilities. The middle class who aspire to live like the monied sector often find that their retirement income runs out and there are few alternatives.

But the system wasn't always this way, and I'm hopeful change will come. Before we look forward to what we can do to fix this distorted structure, let's take a deep dive into the history of how we've cared for our seniors in this country since European colonization. Today's political flashpoints that impact seniors (Medicaid expansion, Social Security solvency, and availability of affordable senior housing) all have their roots in arguments raised and resolved by past generations. These conflicts have resulted in different solutions for the elderly at different times in American history—the proverbial one step forward, two steps back approach we see all too often. Hard fought gains by reformers face back tracking by the established interests. And while we'll find that capitalism hasn't always *completely* run the show, compassionate care has too often been too hard to come by.

ANTEBELLUM AMERICA

Historically, seniors in the United States who had the good fortune to live a long life, lived at home and were cared for by their immediate families. If they didn't have family members who could care for them, the elderly would turn to their village for their care. In the mid nineteenth century, about 70 percent of persons sixty-five or older lived with their children or children-in-law. In addition, about a tenth of the elderly lived with other relatives—mainly grandchildren, siblings, nephews, and nieces. Another tenth lived with non-relatives; most of these were boarders, but some were household heads who kept boarders or servants. In 1850, only 11 percent of the elderly lived alone or with only their spouses, and only 0.7 percent lived in institutions such as almshouses and homes for the aged.[8]

The larger cities of colonial America—Boston, New York, and Philadelphia—were among the first to develop almshouses or poorhouses, which were large institutional settings to care for all types of individuals who could not care for themselves, including the elderly and disabled. The Blockley Almshouse in Philadelphia, constructed in 1731–32, provided the first government-sponsored care of the poor in America, as it offered an infirmary and hospital for the sick and insane, besides housing and feeding the impoverished. Only those in dire need, such as orphans, the very sick, and the elderly were supposed to be admitted. For others in need, the city preferred "out-relief" in the form of small amounts of money, clothing, firewood, and food.[9]

Elizabethan poor laws formed the philosophical underpinnings of the terms upon which seventeenth and early eighteenth century elderly, poor, or disabled were entitled to secure aid. The structure of provisioning aid reflected the religious ideology of the Protestant reformation, which stressed the importance of leading a life of industry, piety, and frugality. The hard-working and prosperous were outward manifestations of God's grace.

Receiving charity was seen as a potential moral hazard, condemning the recipient not only to a life of poverty on earth, but perhaps to eternal damnation. The unworthy, the able-bodied idlers, the vagrants, the drunks, and all who failed to otherwise find work were herded into the poorhouse. However, there was a recognition that some were unable to work through no fault of their own—the permanently disabled, orphans, and the frail elderly were deemed the "worthy" poor, and accommodations were made for their care. The discernment between the worthy and unworthy changed over time and is part of what informs the ongoing swings in policy that currently determine the provision of services to the poor, elderly, and disabled in America.

Prior to the Civil War, the elderly in need of assistance applied to the village or town Overseer of Poor Relief. The poor, the disabled, and the elderly petitioned to receive "outdoor relief." This was a provision of food and fuel provided to families with the goal of keeping the elderly in their home either living on their own or with family. Housing stock was basic, but generally more available even than today, and medical care consisted of what we would term "comfort care," since there were few treatments for chronic illness or disease.

Applicants for "outdoor relief" could be turned away or denied aid. As Wagner wrote, "If Mrs. Jones found herself widowed because her husband was killed in battle, or if Mr. Smith was too old to work on his farm and had no children to work it, both would have no choice but to submit themselves to the will of the overseers of the poor."

The Overseer of Poor Relief was an elected position, and, like today, elected officials came from the ranks of the elite, many of whom had little experience with poverty. The poor and elderly could be denied aid, or other less-desirable options were found for their care.

Boarding out, where farmers and villagers were paid by the local authorities to board the elderly and disabled, was one such alternative option. It was expected that boarders be provided with a place to stay and adequate food and heating. For those who had the capacity to work, there was an expectation that they do so. In some New England towns, the elderly were actually auctioned off to the lowest bidder! This system provided few safeguards for abuse.

According to Wagner, "The results of the auctions varied; some people clearly had the same sponsors, the same family taking the person year after year. But in an extreme case, the widow Sarah

Dill was auctioned off for fourteen years and went to fourteen different households."

While modern sensibilities would be shocked to see granny auctioned off, the idea of the low-cost bidder winning the contract to provide government funded services to the elderly is a best practice for the awarding of Medicaid funds. It is seen as good governance.

The average life expectancy in the antebellum period was thirty-seven. People living into their fifties and later without family to care for them were not a sizeable portion of the population.[10] Like today, most seniors vastly preferred the personal agency that came with the provision of outdoor relief, which enabled them to live independently as opposed to boarding out or placement in the poorhouse. Some opted to enter into the poorhouse only in winter months, when the cold and limited options for work pushed them indoors. At minimum, the poorhouse provided warm, secure housing. The transient nature of the institutionalized population made for a growing concern as the worthy poor including the destitute elderly and mothers with children mixed with vagrants and alcholics. The overseers of the poor were challenged to strike the right balance of making the accommodations comfortable enough for the worthy but limited enough to offer motivation to the more able bodied to leave in search of work.

In the South, meanwhile, the treatment of elderly black chattel slaves varied from paternalistic care to the eventuality of sale or worse, since the value of a slave's life could be recouped through insurance. Historian E.D. Genovese wrote, "As long as the Negro is sound, and worth more than the amount insured, self-interest will prompt the owner to preserve the life of the slave; but, if the slave became unsound and there is little prospect of perfect recovery, *the underwriters cannot expect fair play*—the insurance money is worth more than a slave, and the latter is regarded rather in the light of a super-annuated horse. Genovese also reported that some urban slave holders solved the problem of old, disabled slaves by sending them out to peddle or beg to bring in some income as well as support themselves.[11]

POST-CIVIL WAR

The population applying for relief increased following the Civil War as the dislocations of the war resulted in a significant increase in internal migration, leaving families unable to care for the elderly and disabled. In addition, post-war industrialization was fueled by immigrant labor. While the vast majority of the elderly were still cared for by their families, widows, disabled veterans, and single male immigrants did not have available family members to take care of them in a home setting when they became old and sick. The system of outdoor relief and boarding out did not keep pace with the growing need.

For the middle and upper middle class, in this period we can see the origins of today's faith-based or fraternal organization care homes for seniors. According to Bayview Healthcare's *History of Elder Care*: "As an alternative to state-run institutions for the elderly, fraternal organizations, tradesmen and religious groups began to open nonprofit homes for seniors. Examples of these groups include the German Benevolent Society, the Odd Fellows, Masons and Knights of Columbus. Young members of these groups would pay into a pool that would operate much like a pension plan today. The homes that they operated were often quite nice, and some still operate today."[12]

However, for many, the family, faith, or fraternal ties of the village or township had been stretched, and people needing assistance in larger urban areas or even smaller towns often no longer had the good fortune of robust kinship ties to rely on. The increase in the population needing aid, and the changing composition of this population, created an almost about face in the preference for how to care for the poor, elderly, and disabled. Suddenly, the tension between providing housing and care for the worthy poor and ensuring that the able-bodied would be incentivized to work was challenged by the growing numbers of the indigent and disabled.

Local governments at the time began to favor "group housing" over the prior model of "outdoor welfare."[13] The provision of outdoor welfare or direct subsidies to the poor enabled them to live independently and weakened the social controls imposed by the poorhouse or almshouse. However, the conditions of the poorhouse kept all but the most desperate from seeking their services. The larger almshouses in urban areas were notorious for their history of horrific conditions.

These institutions provided care not only to the elderly but to a broad mix of adults and children. The mix of adults and children, men and women, the mentally ill and physically infirm in group housing created conditions ripe for abuse. There was little medical science could offer in the way of a cure for chronic illness since the discovery of antibiotics, insulin and sulfa drugs was decades away. Contagious diseases easily took hold in these institutional settings.

Dependent upon public funding, poorhouses frequently became a political football with each party eager to show the voters that the poorhouse had been mismanaged in the past, but the current party would provide better fiscal oversight. Politicians employed the tried-and-true methods of exposing any perceived waste and cutting costs to the bone to appeal to fiscally conservative voters. Food, heating, staffing, and building repairs were subject to cost reductions.

It's not difficult to see the parallels between today's issues with institutional senior housing and those of the poorhouse in the nineteenth century. Funding for Medicaid skilled nursing and assisted living beds is subject to the vagaries of politics. The same cost-cutting measures employed in the last century are still being visited upon today's seniors living in institutions. The areas where administrators are looking to save money—food, deferred maintenance, and most importantly staff wages and hours are the same. In addition, today's skilled nursing facility administrators must deal with rising costs for insurance, medicine, and medical devices and the need to show a profit to investors.

Despite the best efforts of nineteenth century administrators and matrons of the poorhouse to cut costs, separate the worthy from the unworthy, and enforce order, the multi-generational, multi-abled population found ways of humanizing their surroundings, challenging the most diligent of rule enforcers and capitalizing on the flexibility of wintering in the almshouse and working in fair weather. The reputation of the poorhouse as a solemn place where dwellers dutifully followed the rules in gratitude for their care was challenged by the historical reality.

In Troutdale, Oregon, just outside of Portland, there's a hotel and concert venue built on the grounds of a former poorhouse. Built in 1911, Edgefield is a three-story brick building with a wide wrap-around porch surrounded by acres of farmland. In what was once the cafeteria for the residents, you can dine on fine farm-to-table fare and drink the wine from Edgefield winery. Walking the halls of the hotel, interspersed with pieces by local artists are photos from the days when the facility was the County Poor Farm. The mix of residents, the work requirement, and the transient nature of the population were all part of the Edgefield experience. Many of the residents, or inmates as they originally were called, supplied the labor for the 300-plus-acre farm. Overseen by a succession of well-seasoned, college-educated farm supervisors, Edgefield considered itself a model of agricultural efficiency and production. The fruit, vegetables, dairy, hogs, and poultry raised on property were sufficient for feeding the population at the poor farm, as well as the county hospital and jail. Many years, surplus quantities were canned and sold on the open market.

At Edgefield, during its seven-decade run as a poor farm, a remarkable array of personalities congregated under its roof: sea captains, captains of industry, schoolteachers, ministers, musicians, loggers, nurses, home builders, homemakers, former slaves, and slave owners. There were Germans, Italians, Japanese, Chinese, Native Americans, African Americans, Catholics, Protestants, Muslims, and Buddhists. Frankie of "Frankie and Johnny" notoriety was there. The nephew of celebrated Confederate General Stonewall Jackson surpassed age one hundred while at Edgefield. The one common thread among them was, at one time (and perhaps others) in their lives, each needed a "leg up."[14]

The very isolation of today's seniors, in contrast to the multigenerational living environment of the nineteenth-century almshouse, is creating a new vulnerability for seniors—out of site and out of mind. With resources already stretched, COVID-19 has been devastating to the vulnerable populations in skilled nursing facilities. Residents of independent living and assisted living institutions were prevented from having visitors during the duration of the quarantine orders. This resulted in months of isolation for vulnerable seniors and reduced ability for families to oversee their care.

Both the structure and the limitations of several modern era programs can be traced back to Reconstruction, a volatile era of United States history. Congress established the basic system of pension laws, known as the General Law pension system, in 1862 to provide pensions to both regular Union Army recruits and volunteers who were disabled as a direct result of military service. The pension program covered African American veterans as well as war widows and their dependents. It was the first major pension program in the U.S. As the promise of Reconstruction was increasingly challenged by the establishment and by white supremacy, racial discrimination ran rampant in the pension system. By 1890, 81 percent of white applicants were approved, compared to 44 percent of black applicants.[15]

Our current healthcare system also can find its origins in the Reconstruction Era and here again, race plays a major role. According to *The Atlantic*, "As German Prime Minister Otto von Bismarck's Health Insurance Bill of 1883 created the first modern national health-care system, and as many other countries moved down the path to truly nationalized, universal health care, America instead largely expanded the existing segregated system of local private providers and religious-based charity care."[16]

In essence, the United States' peculiar, private-based health-care system exists at least in part *because* of the country's commitment to maintaining racial hierarchies. America's developing peculiar, private, decentralized, job-pension-based health-care infrastructure was the only fit for a modernizing society that could not abide black citizens sharing in societal benefits, and one where black workers have often been carved out of the gains of labor entirely."[17]

TURN OF THE CENTURY PROGRESSIVE REFORM

Due to continued improvement and advances in sanitation, healthcare, and nutrition, the number of people living to old age at the turn of the century saw a significant increase from the nineteenth century. People who reached age sixty-five in 1900 could expect to live another ten to twelve years. Those that reached the age of eighty-five could expect to live another four to five years. In fact, the average life expectancy at birth increased by ten years from 1900 to 1930, according to SeniorLiving.org.

The trend toward urbanization also continued. By 1920 the majority of Americans lived in urban areas for the first time in America's history.[18] The family, the predominant unit of care for the elderly, was stressed by this trend. Whereas the elderly living in rural areas were an integral part of the community, contributing to daily family farm life, it was more difficult to care for an elderly dependent in a small, crowded urban setting. Many urban wage workers struggled to care for dependent family members including children, the disabled, and the elderly. For the working class, children and the elderly alike needed to keep working as there were no government supports. Suddenly unemployed and unemployable older men and women could become significant financial burdens on their families. One survey done in New York just prior to the 1929 stock market crash showed that 50 percent or more of people sixty-five and older were dependent on relatives or friends (either living with them or getting financial assistance from them to live somewhere else), 2.5% were living in poorhouses or mental hospitals, and 1-2% were living in private homes for the aged.[19]

Rising inequality and growing social unrest in the late nineteenth century following the financial panics of the 1870s and 1890s was the catalyst for a host of social reform movements, including temperance societies calling for prohibition, women's suffrage leagues, and groups aimed at improving the lives of the poor, including orphans, the disabled, and the mentally ill. Advocates for children and for the mentally disabled worked to create alternatives to life in the poorhouse for these populations. Religious and charity groups created orphanages and homes for unwed mothers. Slowly, poorhouses became more and more like elder-care facilities. By the 1920s, nearly 70 percent of almshouse residents were elderly poor.[20]

As the population of aging adults grew due to advances in sanitation and medical science, and the growing urbanization of America stressed families to care for their elderly dependents, individuals and families looked to the government for support. The origins of the modern pension and healthcare systems began more fully developing during the Progressive era.

At this time, pensions were becoming more common but far from universal. By 1900, only one-fifth of all white men fifty-five and older could rely on a pension.[21] States only offered limited assistance to a growing indigent elderly population. However, to qualify for benefits, the ability of the extended family to pay was taken into account. What were the poor and working-class elderly to do? The answer was to keep working. In this era children, immigrants, women, and the elderly were needed to fuel American industry. Wage labor was often dirty, dangerous, and incredibly taxing. The eight-hour workday was not law until for most industries until the Fair Labor Standards Act was passed as part of the New Deal in the 1940s. The elderly were one of the populations that served as excess labor pool standing ready to take undesirable work, flexibly expand and contract with labor demand, and to work for low wages with the expectation that the extended family would provide for their care.

It was the private sector which recognized the need for support to families in caring for their elderly and infirm dependents. The Metropolitan Life Insurance Company created a pool of visiting nurses in order to reduce the risk they incurred by the premature death of a policy holder. Those who could afford a policy were eligible for home care provided by a growing cadre of visiting nurses. Advances in medical care and increased opportunities for women to be educated and employed made this a popular service for the middle class. With visiting nurses filling the need, the United States failed to enact a comprehensive system to provision healthcare for all its citizens. The patchwork and local system of private and charity hospitals was strained to care for a growing and urbanized population.

While Progressive reformers were successful in securing the vote for women, legislating sanitation regulations, and enacting labor reforms, they failed to make any progress toward a comprehensive system of healthcare. The cries of "socialized medicine" and "rationing" that we hear today echo back to the turn of the century. The pushback from doctors against a comprehensive system of the provision of healthcare could be seen to be part of the agenda for physicians to professionalize their ranks and confer status and exclusivity on the role of doctor. Physicians were looking to establish themselves as credentialed and separate from the host of homeopaths, midwives and folk medicine practitioners which had long been the sources of medical care and comfort in the United States. Following the recommendations of a report authored by educator Abraham Flexner, medical education became standardized, and states began to license physicians.

The impact of these changes on the provision of healthcare further bifurcated the provision of healthcare in America by race and class. As a result of the Flexner report, all but two of the historically black medical schools and six of the seven medical schools for women were closed. The push toward licensing and standardization pushed out the quacks hawking tonics and elixirs and but also midwives, folk healers, neuropaths, and scores of practitioners serving the poor and working class providing some level of preventive care and healing. Access to medical care in the United States became limited and more expensive with the emphasis on specialization, surgery, and pharmaceuticals that we see today.

THE GREAT DEPRESSION AND THE NEW DEAL

In the Progressive Era, while Americans could look forward to living longer, there were few supports to take care of aging adults. A growing number of members of the middle class benefitted from pensions and insurance which provided cash payments and health services including the provision of visiting nurses. For those who needed additional care, religious and fraternal organizations provided a comfortable setting for their affiliates. However, for the poor and working class, the only option for many older adults was to work until they expired. Medical advances and the professionalization of physicians lengthened the lifespan for Americans overall, but there was no universal or comprehensive health delivery system. African Americans and women were excluded from the newly accredited medical schools and licensing requirements for physicians. The poor and working class lost access to the midwives and folk healers that they had relied upon. This separate and unequal system was sorely tested in the Great Depression of the 1930s causing untold suffering for many Seniors.

Seniors were one of the populations hit hardest by the stock market crash of 1929 and the ensuing Great Depression. Retirees with assets saw them evaporate overnight as the stock market crash virtually wiped out all of the gains made during the Roaring Twenties. Even prudent savers could have lost their nest eggs overnight. When a bank closed, a worker's life savings were completely gone. It would not be until the Banking Act of 1935 was passed as part of the New Deal legislation, that the government would insure bank deposits.

With unemployment as high as 40 percent in some areas of the country, many older adults lost their jobs. The poverty rate among those 65 and older exceeded 50 percent, according to some sources. Many extended family networks split up as wage earners took the road to find employment. Children were boarded out with other relatives. And the elderly were often left to fend for themselves or ended up in the poorhouse. Charities were stretched to their limits as soup kitchen lines stretched for blocks. Like today, people without housing took to constructing tent camps, or Hoovervilles.

My children's paternal grandfather and grandmother were among the many who came to California from the ecological disaster of the dustbowl in the Midwest during the Great Depression. Pauline worked packing peaches in Sanger California, while Archie worked for Western Union delivering telegrams on a bicycle on the hilly streets of San Francisco as a seventeen-year-old. Archie recounted hunting squirrels in the hills to bring home to feed the family. My mother's immigrant Maltese family relied on a large kitchen garden, raising rabbits and chickens, and bartering within their community. My grandfather was fortunate to have kept his job as a warehouseman in San Francisco during the Depression. My paternal grandfather lost his job in 1929, forcing my father to drop out of school at age twelve to aid in supporting the family.

In Troutdale Oregon, the population of the Edgefield Poor House swelled to more than six hundred in the Depression: "Closets were converted and residents put three or more to a room in an ongoing effort to accommodate the great demand. The poor farm's basement quickly emerged as a veritable bazaar made up of booths operated by the legions of unemployed craftsmen and artisans living upstairs. The pool of talent and services available in those basement booths drew faithful patronage from Portland customers."[22]

At the time the Great Depression began, the United States was the only industrialized country in the world without some form of unemployment insurance or social security. Grassroots movements sprung up across the country. Charismatic leaders developed nationwide followings and progressive political parties posed a real challenge to the establishment parties. The Communist Party, and the International Workers of the World (IWW) were strong advocates for labor reforms and for the enactment of a Social Welfare State. The threat of Communism to American capitalism was real since the Russian Revolution of 1918. The Communist Party made inroads in organizing for labor rights, forming labor councils, organizing hunger strikes, and supporting African American empowerment. The apex of Communist led organizing was the San Francisco General Strike of 1934. Beginning with longshoremen and dock workers, the City of San Francisco and one of the largest ports on the West Coast was shut down for over two months.

The governor of Louisiana from 1928-1932, Huey Long, left flanked President Roosevelt within the Democratic Party, pressuring the centrist leader to enact larger government intervention to address the ravages of the Depression. Long's proposal the "Share Our Wealth" Program called for massive federal spending, a wealth tax, and a wealth distribution plan. Americans across the county participated in Share Our Wealth groups. By 1935, the society had over 7.5 million members in 27,000 clubs across the country. Long's plan called for the institution of a guaranteed basic household income, a $30 monthly pension for those over sixty-five, and free medical care.

Francis Townsend and his Townsend Plan was focused specifically on addressing the needs of the elderly poor. The plan stipulated that every person older than sixty be paid $200 per month.

Furthermore, the Old-Age Revolving Pension fund was to be supported by a 2 percent national sales tax. Recipients had to be retired, free from habitual criminality, and must spend the money within thirty days to further stimulate the economy. Like the Share Our Wealth clubs, more than 3,400 Townsend plan clubs were meeting across the United States to pressure the government to enact an old age insurance program.

Sinclair Lewis, the muckraking journalist who exposed the horrors of the meat packing industry in his seminal book *The Jungle*, ran for governor of California in 1934. His plan, End Poverty in California (EPIC) called for implementation of a progressive income tax, imposition of an inheritance tax, a massive public works program, and an old-age pension program. Like Long and Townsend, Lewis popularized his plan through the implementation of local End Poverty Leagues.

While these parties and individuals were ultimately unsuccessful in implementing their plans, the combined pressure and the specter of the elderly living in Hoovervilles and eating out of trash cans prompted the Roosevelt Administration to enact the Social Security Act in 1935.

Social Security

The Social Security Act was initially proposed by the Roosevelt Administration and passed by Congress in 1935. While it provided for cash payments to the elderly, reducing poverty, and providing an option to a lifetime of work, it fell far short of a European-style social welfare state. Title 1 of the Act included two parts—the Old Age Assistance Program (OAA), which was designed to give immediate cash payments to the low-income elderly and the Old Age Insurance (OAI) program, which relied on payroll deductions to build up a reserve from which future payments would be made.

The first OAI payment was not scheduled be paid out until seven years later in 1942.

The OAA, the immediate cash assistance component of the legislation, was basically federal support for existing State programs. According to SeniorLiving.org, "Each state was allowed to set its own standards for determining eligibility and payments, with the federal government providing cash for a 50% match of up to $30 a month in aid. The lack of federal control was deliberate. The legislation was written that way to get the support of states that wanted the federal government's assistance without too many strings attached." The limitations of the state-run programs carried into the OAA. The federal government did impose a light level of standardization ensuring the program was available in every county and that people sixty-five and older were eligible to receive benefits. Some of the onerous state level limitations persisted in some areas including means tests for the families of applicants.[23]

Another significant omission of the OAA was payments to the elderly who resided in poorhouses. Once again, the pendulum was swinging back from institutionalizing the elderly to supporting them in residing in the community. Part of the consideration was that the poorhouses had been overrun with applicants during the Depression and there was little political will for new construction. However, the need for housing the elderly who needed assistance did not go away. Housing provided by religious and fraternal organizations could not expand quickly enough to meet the need and donors wanted to keep the institutions limited to their members.

Boarding in private homes quickly became the preferred option. Boarding out the elderly was not a new phenomenon. In colonial times, the village paid farmers and small holders to house the dependent elderly. The scale of boarding out met the moment. Private homeowners were happy to accept OAA recipients as boarders since they were a ready source of reliable cash in a time of great need. My partner's maternal grandmother took in three boarders in her rural Kansas home even though there was only one bathroom with a family of seven living in the home. Boarders made it possible for homeowners to hang onto their home while others fell victim to evictions and sheriff sales. Many of the private residences housing the elderly were run by unemployed nurses giving rise to a cottage industry of private nursing homes.

The Social Security Act created a separate program for the poor who were not elderly. This separation harkens back to earlier concern about separating the worthy from the unworthy poor. The elderly were seen as worthy of assistance. In the height of the Great Depression, there was also an economic argument in favor of allowing older workers to retire, creating the opportunity for younger workers, especially male heads of household, to have a job.

The second component of Title 1 of the Social Security Act was the OAI—Old Age Insurance Program. This program was not means tested and was funded through payroll deductions. This singularly successful program has resulted in a significant reduction in senior poverty and is very politically popular even today. At the time of its inception, however, there were significant limitations. For instance, job categories not covered by the act included workers in agricultural labor, domestic service, government employees, and many teachers, nurses, hospital employees, librarians, and social workers. The Social Security payroll tax is also a regressive tax since there is a cap on the income that is subject to the payroll deduction ensuring that lower-income workers pay a higher percentage of their salary into Social Security.

The Great Depression imprinted a generation of Americans. My grandparents were not unique as they hoarded cash in their mattress and kept every little thing with the expectation that even a pencil stub or a jar could be needed at some time. The severe depravation and grassroots political pressure finally prompted government action to create a systematic program of cash payments for the poor and the elderly. These programs were not universal with segments of the population left out entirely or subject to stringent state level limitations. The repercussions of the political compromises which favored State level control can still be felt today as States block Medicaid expansion leaving hundreds of thousands of Americans without access to healthcare. State control of budgets for programs supporting the elderly including In-Home Supportive Services (IHSS) leave these programs vulnerable to budget cuts and local imposition of onerous requirements. Unlike European Social Welfare states, no provision was made during the New Deal for the provision of universal medical care. Cash payments to individual seniors enabled the growth of a cottage industry of boarding homes in the community, emptying out the poorhouse and giving rise to the emerging private-for-profit nursing home.

POST WAR

The Post War period saw the greatest continued expansion of the economy with sustained economic growth and rising living standards. The United States emerged from the Second World War as an unchallenged industrial powerhouse. The post-war boom was fueled by a progressive tax structure and considerable federal investment in infrastructure including the building of hospitals. Significant legislation was passed to expand Social Security, create standards for the provision of healthcare and ultimately to enact the Medicare and Medicaid programs. What is also significant are the gaps that this legislation engendered and the failure to create a comprehensive social safety net for our elderly and especially those most in need.

Cash Payments

The OAA (the Old Age Assistance Program), while providing much needed income, continued to be implemented at the state level, leaving uneven support. While the federal government was picking up 60 percent of the cost, State budgets were stretched to cover the remaining costs in the face of the growing rolls. As the OAI (Old Age Insurance) program began making payments in 1942, states moved to migrate the elderly from the OAA to the OAI in order to minimize the rolls and state payments.

States were also aggressive in ensuring that seniors met the means test for the OAA. OAA payments were to be reserved for the needy. Seniors trying to access state payments were subject to intrusive scrutiny as workers looked to identify other available means of support including any small gifts by families or even the output of a kitchen garden.

The OAI, or what we know now as Social Security, was modified several times in the 1950s with each modification expanding eligibility. According to SeniorLiving.org: "Several amendments to the Social Security Act were made in the 1950's, creating millions of additional people who would have a reliable source of income in their old age. In 1950, domestic workers; farm workers; non-farm, non-professional self-employed persons; and federal civilian employees not in the federal retirement system were brought into Social Security. In 1951, railroad workers with less than 10 years of service were added. In 1954, homeworkers and all self-employed persons except lawyers and medical professionals became eligible. In 1956, members of the military and all remaining self-employed persons except doctors joined."

Pensions

The post-war period was also the golden age for pensions. According to a CNBC article, "Until the 1980s, most Americans planned for retirement through pensions. They were defined-benefit plans, in which employers saved on workers' behalf and calculated employees' retirement benefits based on their years of service and final salary."[24]

The 401k was introduced by Congress with the passage of the Revenue Act of 1978. The 401k was supposed to offer employees who had a pension a choice and to broaden the opportunities for people to save for retirement who were not covered by a pension plan. The idea of offering choice masked the intent of Fortune 500 companies who lobbied hard for the passage of the act. With the passage of the act and the introduction of the 401k, the burden of risk shifted from companies that had needed to properly fund and administer a pension plan on behalf of their retired employees to the employees themselves. Quickly, the percentage of American retirees covered by a pension declined from the high of 60 percent in the 1980s to less than 13 percent today. Seniors are now left to navigate the vagaries of the stock market on their own and are solely responsible for making the investment decisions that will impact them for the rest of their lives.

With the shift into 401k plans taking over, "workers' retirement prospects are increasingly affected by economic downturns. Much of the 401(k) era coincided with rising stock and housing prices that propped up family wealth measures even as the savings rate declined. This house of cards collapsed in 2000–2001 and again in 2007–2009. In 2013 most families still had not recovered their losses from the financial crisis and Great Recession, let alone accumulated additional savings for retirement," according to an EPI report. In addition, the report also shows that the transition from defined benefit plans to defined contribution plans (401k) greatly exacerbated the racial wealth gap. (13) Black workers' participation in employer-based retirement plans used to be similar to that of white workers, but black workers began lagging behind white workers in the 401(k) era, while Hispanic workers fell even further behind. For families with retirement account savings, the median amount is $22,000 for black and Hispanic families, compared with $73,000 for white non-Hispanic families."[25]

Women are the other group which has not fared well in the transition away from pensions. Lower earnings and lower retirement savings rates have led to a large disparity in the median 401k balances of women compared to men. Baby Boomer women have a median 401k savings balance of $59,000, far less than half of the $138,000 median balance of Boomer men, according to a recent T. Rowe Price survey.[26]

Healthcare

Significantly, a comprehensive program to provide a system of healthcare was omitted from the Social Security legislation. In 1943, Congress took up the Wagner-Murray-Dingell bill, which, if passed, would have implemented a "federally sponsored health insurance program, along with permanent and temporary disability, maternity and death benefits, full federalization of the existing Federal-State unemployment insurance, expansion of old-age and survivors' insurance, and enlargement of public assistance."[27] Again, the American Medical Association strongly lobbied against the bill. Although the Wagner-Murray-Dingell Bill generated extensive national debates, with the intensified opposition, the bill never passed by Congress despite its reintroduction every session for fourteen years! Had it passed, the Act would have established compulsory national health insurance funded by payroll taxes.

President Harry Truman was a strong supporter of a national health insurance program. He was moved to create a comprehensive program noting that the rich could avail themselves of private insurance programs and quality care and charities existed to serve the poor, although this safety net was full of holes. Truman was most concerned about the middle class. Truman wrote, "I am trying to fix it so the people in the middle-income bracket can live as long as the very rich and the very poor."[28]

In the Cold War era following World War II, the American Medical Association played upon the nation's fear of Communism to challenge Truman's support for a national health insurance program. This type of red baiting argument was persuasive with Republicans and conservative Southern Democrats. In addition, the needs of the middle class were increasingly addressed by private insurance companies and for the working class through healthcare benefits offered to union members. Public programs continued to be associated with a failure of personal and family responsibility and an affront to personal freedom.

An investment in America's infrastructure was an enduring legacy of the Truman administration. The Hill-Burton Act of 1946 funded a dramatic expansion of our nation's hospital system. Hill-Burton federal funding was used to build and expand hospitals in poor and rural areas and to upgrade hospitals in urban areas. While Hill-Burton funding could not be used by for-profit hospitals, it was approved for use by non-profit organizations as well as public entities. This infusion of federal funds resulted in the construction of hundreds of new hospitals and nursing care homes.

While the capacity to care for the elderly increased, the quality of these care institutions varied widely. The Hill-Burton legislation included safety standards for institutions receiving these funds, but these standards covered only a small percentage of the growing population of nursing and care homes. Another issue for the elderly and their families was how to pay for medical and institutional care? Unable to pass a comprehensive program, Congress incrementally updated the existing OAA legislation.

Available federal funding swung the pendulum toward institutionalization of the elderly. Support for the elderly to live at home or with their families continued to be the responsibility of State and local government. I n 1965, Congress passed the Older Americans Act, creating what came to be called the "Aging Network," a web of federal, state, and local agencies linked together to focus on social services and other programs primarily targeted to older adults living in their homes. The mission of the Aging Network expanded in numerous ways over the years. It began to include advocacy efforts, meal programs, and a number of other services. Due to funding shortfalls, many of the services developed long waiting lists, however, limiting the benefits to a relatively small proportion of the poorest elderly. The legacy of this legislative funding patchwork can be experienced today with underfunded and patchy support for seniors to age safely in their homes.

Medicare and Medicaid

After years of tinkering around the edges of the New Deal programs, Lyndon Johnson was able to work with Congress to pass Medicare. Amendments passed to the Social Security Act in 1965 established the Medicare and Medicaid programs, with Medicare Part A covering hospital costs, and Part B being a voluntary program partially financed by premiums that covered physician and other out-of-hospital costs. An existing federal program, Kerr-Mills, was converted to Medicaid to cover the impoverished elderly.

The enactment of Medicare was done as part of Lyndon Johnson's Great Society programs in response to the intensive political pressure brought to bear by Civil Rights groups including anti-poverty advocates. Like during the New Deal, a charismatic president leveraged the political pressure from grassroots organizations to overcome the pushback from the establishment. However, Medicare legislation and its implementation at the State level contained the gaps and engendered the consequences that today trap the infirm elderly in institutional care, require the elderly to spend down into poverty to receive long term care and leave gaps in the American healthcare system which bankrupt thousands of Americans and result in premature death for others who cannot access care. Implementation of these federal programs at the State level also permitted the Southern States to continue with racial segregated health care delivery.

Immediately, the problems with the legislation were clear. The federally budget for Medicaid blew past all budget expectations. States quickly moved to shut down any remaining state-funded institutions moving their charges to Medicaid funded beds in nursing homes. The infirm elderly who may have benefitted from in-home support quickly found out that the only way to get care was to move into a nursing home. At Edgefield, the last remaining residents were moved into nursing homes and the facility was ultimately shuttered for decades.

In order to reduce costs, the federal government in the late 1960s moved to aggressively deny eligibility. With eligibility determination taking weeks if not months, families were left holding the bag if their elderly relative's claim was denied. According to SeniorLiving.org, denial rates shot up more than 600 percent between early 1968 and early 1970. Even as families struggled to qualify for benefits, someone was getting rich. The 1970s saw the growth of publicly traded networks of nursing and care homes promising investors returns of 20 to 25 percent a year."[29]

THE MORAL HAZARDS OF PRIVATIZATION

In her 1974 expose, *Tender Loving Greed*, author Mary Adelaide Mendelson cites numerous instances of wide-spread corruption and exploitation in the elder care industry. Looking backward at the long struggle to enact Medicare and Medicaid in the face of establishment pushback, Mendelson cites the nature of what she terms the fatal compromise: "What did come out of the long struggle over federal health insurance were programs under which Washington poured money into the health industry with a minimum of regulation of how that money was used. In effect, the sponsors of Medicaid and Medicare said to the industry: 'Let us give you the money, and we won't look too closely at how it is spent.' That fatal compromise is the root cause of the nursing home industry's ability to extract excess profits from the government."[30]

The moral hazards of our private-for-profit health care industry cited in Mendelson's expose run the gamut from petty scams taking grandma's spending money, to overcharging and receiving kickbacks from suppliers to the big money payoffs in the stock market enabled by corporate shell structures and tax manipulation. For-profit elder care homes, including independent living, assisted living, memory care and skilled nursing facilities, are big business and exist to make a profit for shareholders. Like the privatization of pensions, our privatized healthcare system generates profits for investors yet leaves the seniors who need regular income and healthcare to fend for themselves.

Today, many senior care facilities are publicly traded corporations organized as Real Estate Investment Trusts (REITs). While the investor class can count on generous dividend payouts from REITs that manage senior living facilities, the seniors in these facilities are vulnerable to cost cutting measures that can result in illness or death, as we saw far too often during the COVID-19 pandemic.

The size of these corporations and trusts for senior living facilities is significant. Consider Sunrise Senior Living, a McLean, Virginia-based company that employs approximately 32,000 people. As of June 1, 2019, Sunrise operated three hundred and twenty-seven communities in the United States, Canada, and the United Kingdom, including twenty-one Gracewell Healthcare communities, with a total unit capacity of approximately 29,300 residents. In 2019, REIT eldercare giant REIT Welltower announced its purchase of five Sunrise properties in which it had previously been an investor. Sunrise would continue to manage the properties, "under and incentive-based management contract."[31]

The management challenges for a large corporation like Sunrise are significant indeed, and investment advisors acknowledge an obvious risk associated with investment in these REITs. According to a 2020 Seeking Alpha article, "Those nursing home costs are far more than most retirees can handle. The option is there for those who can afford it, but many simply don't have the money. If you're trying to survive on a smaller income, you avoid paying out $100k/year for as long as possible."[32] From an investor perspective, increased regulation is also seen as a potential threat to growth.

From a workforce standpoint, REIT-managed nursing homes are failing as well, as corporations turn increasingly to AI-driven screening tools to handle mass staff turnovers and fill perceived employee performance gaps.[33] Low pay for workers tending to our elderly relatives is seen as a challenge to overcome with AI enhanced software, not an issue to be addressed with increased wages. Meanwhile, in 2012, when Sunrise was acquired by Healthcare REIT, Sunrise CEO Mark Ordan earned over $16 million.[34]

The 2019 Tax Code reform was a boon to REIT investors. "One of the central features of the tax bill is a new 20 percent deduction on pass-through income. This deduction applies to businesses that operate as pass-through entities, REITs included. "REITs are mandated to distribute at least 90 percent of their income, and REITs do not pay taxes on this distributed income," says Austin Pickle, investment strategy analyst for Wells Fargo Investment Institute in Sarasota, Florida in a Yahoo News article.[35] Pass-through income gets a big tax break. This means REITs generally don't owe any taxes!

Beyond the dangers of REIT-driven management groups, institutional living became a breeding ground for the super spread of COVID-19 during the global pandemic. Seniors in congregant living make up the highest percentage of Americans who have died from COVID. However, even in the face of this tragedy, the Welltower's CEO had reason to remain optimistic, telling the press: "In the Great Recession, occupancy declined and access to capital was constricted. However, the sector proved resilient—particularly assisted living, as a needs-based product. Already, other leaders in the sector, including Welltower CEO Tom DeRosa, have said that COVID-19 could in fact prove the value of senior living to consumers, who will see the benefits of high quality care and robust infection control. In the longer term, COVID-19 does not change the demographics that are working in favor of senior housing and care."[36]

These remarks by Mr. De Rosa reflect a fundamental truth. Despite the ravages of COVID-19, there remains a huge need for better services for our growing population of seniors who need some level support in managing their activities of daily living or who need medical care. With the support of a generous tax code for for-profit investors encouraging the development of large, corporate entities, there are limited other options. Many seniors, like my mother, truly believed that they were doing the right thing for themselves and for their families in moving into private-for-profit congregant living facilities.

In an attempt to address the crisis of long-term care for the dependent elderly, a national long-term care insurance program was introduced as part of the Affordable Care Act by President Obama's administration in 2010. The premise of the CLASS Act was to create a government option for long-term care insurance. However, program success would be dependent on a wide range of purchasers including not only the old and sick but the young and healthy. Realistically the only way to achieve this outcome was through mandated participation—the very same mandates that made the ACA (Obamacare) so politically unpopular. The CLASS Act (Community Living Assistance Security and Support program) never got off the ground and was officially terminated in 2011.

The introduction and subsequent failure of the CLASS Act clearly reflects the extent to which privatization has eclipsed comprehensive government funded solutions for eldercare. At the time, Mitch McConnell surmised that the failure of the CLASS Act was an indicator that the Affordable Care Act (Obamacare) would also fail. He would spend the next ten years trying to make this a reality.

There is little political will to create a comprehensive, government-supported, long-term-care program. In addition, Medicare, the successful and popular government managed healthcare program for seniors, has become increasingly privatized through programs like Medicare Advantage, a private plan alternative to traditional Medicare. According to a report by KFF, "In 2021, more than 26 million people were enrolled in a Medicare Advantage plan, accounting for 42 percent of the total Medicare population, and $343 billion (or 46 percent) of total federal Medicare spending (net of premiums)."[37]

Under Medicare Advantage, beneficiaries use their Medicare benefit to buy a private plan. Medicare pays insurers a benchmark rate based on traditional Medicare spending in a geographic region, enabling plans to offer benefits outside of fee-for-service such as dental or vision benefits. Some Medicare Advantage plans even offer free gym membership or meal delivery. Many younger and healthier seniors are able to pay less however older and sicker seniors may end up paying much more or finding they are unable to get the specialty care they need. Medicare Advantage plans limit access to physicians in a geographic area and require referrals before seeing a specialist. Any initial cost savings with a Medicare Advantage plan can be quickly overcome later in life when seriously ill seniors have to pay out of pocket.

Medicare Advantage plans are big business. Humana, one of the larger providers, noted in its 2021 fourth quarter earnings report that they will be investing $ 1 billion to try and capture growing market share as Boomers become Medicare eligible.[38] Established insurers like Humana and United Healthcare are facing competition from venture funded start-ups as Wall Street, and the investor class has recognized the outsized profits to be made from Medicare Advantage offerings. Investors see the federal government funded program as a cash cow. Insurers get money from the government, spend less than traditional Medicare on actual services, and enrich themselves and investors with the difference.

Biden's proposed Build Back Better plan would have invested in traditional Medicare, enabling the popular program to offer hearing and dental benefits similar to Medicare Advantage plans. However, Congress did not pass this legislation, and many point to the influence that insurance companies have in Washington.

POLICY IMPLICATIONS

Looking back at the history of elder care in the United States lays bare the limitations of our capitalist system in caring for members who are not actively productive. From colonial times until today, when a Senior was unable to generate a paycheck, other means were identified to monetize them. Colonial Americans auctioned off the impoverished elderly to small holders and villagers who were reimbursed for their care. Today, monetizing the elderly is big business with Real Estate Investment Trusts and Medicare Advantage programs generating millions in profits for executives and investors, while seniors struggle under the system. As 401Ks have replaced defined-benefit pension plans, seniors have increasingly aged into poverty as investor profits have soared.

The U.S. political class is also very attuned to the moral hazards associated with subsidizing healthcare, including long-term care and cash payments to the poor and the elderly. A little more than one hundred years ago it was morally acceptable to have the elderly work until they dropped. Social Security and Medicare were hard won achievements by grassroots organizations putting pressure on politicians during times of great economic and political unrest.

No battle is ever truly over, and our generation must remain vigilant against the establishment push back and threats of takeaways. Raids on the Social Security trust fund are commonplace, and expansion of Medicaid under the Affordable Care Act was rejected by Conservative politicians in many states where the need for healthcare is overwhelming. The Build Back Better legislation was scuttled in the Senate with pressure from insurers. Concessions to Southern Democrats and other establishment conservatives were at the root of the failure to enact a comprehensive system for healthcare delivery. Delegation of the implementation of Medicare and Medicaid to the States allowed for racial segregation of health services to continue. Left to set their own priorities, States continue to shortchange budgets for senior nutrition, home health, and other services to support seniors living in their homes and there is very little political will in Washington to enact systemic change

History shows that the pendulum has swung back and forth between institutionalizing seniors and providing support to allow seniors to live safely at home in their communities. From colonial era poorhouses to today's senior living centers, institutional living has afforded a high degree of social control and was seen as a cost cutting measure. The pendulum has also swung the other way, with boarding out and cash payments supporting the elderly to live at home or in the community.

Whatever the dominant model of the time, such situations are highly dependent on good caregivers to function in a way that actually serve our seniors needs. Caregivers and the provision of other home-based services are key to allowing seniors to safely continue to live at home rather than in an institution.

As we'll see in the next chapter, which focuses on caregivers, caring for our seniors is largely a female led activity. Whether it be paid caregivers or family members, the vast majority of those who care for the elderly are women. Without comprehensive government supported social programs, the elderly population relies on their daughters and other women to care for them in their homes. The impact of being a caregiver has long-term impacts on employment, wages, savings, and health for those giving care and significant gaps for those who depend on them.

CHAPTER THREE

WHO GIVES CARE?

At one point, wages for my mother's caregivers overcame housing as her biggest expense. That was certainly true when Mary began living in the little trailer. But the wages for her caregivers combined with medical insurance, co-pays for doctor's visits, medication, and uncovered medical expenses (including diapers) grew increasingly expensive during her final years in the independent living facilities. This growing increase in medical expenses, and the reliance on caregivers, depleted Mary's nest egg shockingly fast. It was one of the critical factors that ultimately forced her move into the trailer and later to the Medicaid-funded, skilled nursing facility.

Much like childcare workers, those who care for seniors are largely female, undervalued, and underpaid. Concurrent with the growing crisis of seniors falling into poverty is the existing crisis of women who are experiencing poverty themselves caring for our seniors. In this chapter, we'll explore the demographics of who serves as caregivers and why and look at the imbalanced socioeconomic portrait of the caregiving industry.

THE GROWING DEMAND FOR CARE

As humans, we cannot predict the future, and we certainly cannot predict the hour or the circumstances of our passing. One of the biggest challenges of ensuring that we can adequately care for ourselves and our loved ones at the end of their lives is the sheer variability of the level of care needed and the duration. Many of us choose to be optimistic, believing that we will be healthy to the end, or that our care requirements will be minimal. Many Americans believe that Medicare will pay for an extended stay in a skilled nursing facility should the need arise. That is simply not the case.

While we cannot predict our individual circumstances, there is a lot we do know about the care needs for seniors overall. Today's aging baby boomers are living longer and in poorer health than the Greatest Generation that preceded them. Some seniors may need very little care until end-of-life support; others may require years of care to support the most basic and intimate needs of daily life.

Let's look at some statistics that come from LongTermCare. Gov, a U.S. Government website:

- Someone turning age 65 today has almost a 70 percent chance of needing some type of long-term care services and supports in their remaining years

- Women need care longer (3.7 years) than men (2.2 years)

- One-third of today's 65-year-olds may never need long-term care support, but 20 percent will need it for longer than five years.[39]

These are sobering statistics. One in five seniors will need long-term care for longer than five years! For middle class seniors, the looming issue is who will provide the care needed and who will pay for it. The wealthy can employ paid caregivers and enjoy the benefits of institutional living in resort-like settings. For the poor, Medicaid is the fund source for end-of life-care. While Medicaid has its issues, a senior needing skilled nursing care can find a bed in a facility. It may not be close to home or in the most desirable facility, but it's a bed, nonetheless. For the vast majority of those in the middle, the senior care needs may be simply out of reach financially.

A recent study projects that "by 2029 there will be 14.4 million middle-income seniors, 60 percent of whom will have mobility limitations and 20 percent of whom will have high health care and functional needs. While many of these seniors will likely need the level of care provided in senior housing, we project that 54 percent of seniors will not have sufficient financial resources to pay for it."[40]

The majority of those needing long term care are women. Any visit to a skilled nursing facility will corroborate this; the hallways are lined with women in wheelchairs. According to Nancy E. Shurtz, a professor at the University of Oregon Law School, "Women have an increased need for long term care because of their increased life expectancy and their increased risk of developing chronic ailments like Alzheimer's disease. Women generally outlive men by five or more years. Women aged 65 today can expect to live twenty more years and require an average of 3.7 years of extended long term care support."[41]

These are conservative estimates, and the conclusions echo my mother's experience. As my mother aged, the consequences of living with Type 2 diabetes took a toll on her, resulting in the need for stepped-up levels of care which she was increasingly unable to pay for. Complications from diabetes compromised her vision, her kidney functioning, and her vascular capacity resulting in mobility and cognitive decline.

In the last five years of her life, of the six basic ADLs—eating, bathing, getting dressed, toileting, transferring, and continence—my mother needed assistance with five: bathing, getting dressed, toileting, transferring and continence. While my mother was able to feed herself, she needed daily assistance in preparing meals and help to get groceries. In addition, she needed assistance with medication management, managing her finances, transportation, maintaining a clean house, laundry, and support in interacting with healthcare and social services systems.

The need for assistance was gradual and grew over time. However, illness and injury resulted in intermittent needs for increased care during the period of rehabilitation. For *fifteen* years before her death, Mary needed assistance with housecleaning, meal preparation and transportation. The independent living facilities provided these services. For *ten* years she needed additional assistance with bathing, medication management, laundry, financial management and help with doctor's visits. In assisted living, this level of care was provided by the facility with my support for doctor visits.

In the last three years of her life, my mother transitioned from independent living facilities to the trailer, to skilled nursing. When living independently, paid caregivers provided assistance with bathing, getting dressed, toileting, transferring and continence, as well as laundry and housecleaning. I managed grocery shopping, financial management, all healthcare and social service visits, and the purchasing of health care supplies and medications.

Many of the stresses and trade-offs I experienced with my caring for my mother were familiar. I have always been a working mother and was a single parent and primary provider from the time my children were in early elementary school. As hard as those days were, I found that caring for my mother was much harder. Balancing her care needs with my job and caring for my family was harder still.

WHO GIVES CARE?

The role of a caregiver is vital. They support our seniors to successfully live at home and in their communities, avoiding the significant disadvantages of institutional living. In families, this role almost exclusively performed by daughters. While feminists may have made some inroads in increasing male participation in housework and child care, elder care is a final frontier in the gender wars. More than 65 percent of older people who need long-term care rely solely on family and friends, and most of those caregivers—estimates range from 59 to 75 percent—are women, according to the Family Caregiver Alliance[42]. A recent study by a Princeton researcher found that daughters step up twice as often as sons, regardless of job status, child-care duties, and other variables[43] [44].

Paid caregiving is largely a female dominated occupation with high stress, high turnover and low pay. In California, one of the richest states in the country, most paid caregivers are women of color. According to salary.com the average salary for a home health aide in California in 2022 is around $29,518 per year. Even in New York City, the average rate of pay for a home health aide is $15.93 per hour, falling behind a living wage of $21.77. Furthermore, most paid caregivers there are women of color, a consistently oppressed, marginalized, and under-compensated demographic in our country. The wages are so low that nearly 20 percent of care workers live in poverty, and more than 40 percent rely on some form of public assistance.

Our society does not value those who give care. Low or no pay and high stress characterize the lives of caregivers creating a significant risk for those who are giving care to ultimately end up needing the very care they had been providing. Disability and poverty are perpetuated as the very result of their role as caregivers. Unpaid and low wage caregivers can jeopardize their own health and secure retirement caring for the dependent elderly. This cycle that combines economically undervalued labor with pernicious long-term effects on future financial stability helps to perpetuate and exacerbate the feminization of poverty. Feminist theorist Martha Chamallas calls this situation a "double bind" where the interests of those requiring care stand in opposition to those administering care. There is an underlying conflict between the needs of the dependent elderly and the unpaid or poorly compensated care provider. Let's take a moment to look at the groups who are most often tasked with caretaking and honor the challenges they face themselves—baby boomers, daughters and wives, and low wage caregivers.

BABY BOOMERS

As a member of the Baby Boom generation (those born between 1946 and 1964) and a female, I am part of the largest cohort of caregivers in the United States. The stress I felt as I stretched between caring for my mother, working, and caring for my children and partner are all too common for caregivers. I experienced the" double bind" where caring for my mother had a negative impact on caring for myself and for the others who were dependent on me.

The health outlook for my generation is not good. According to a 2020 CDC report, Baby Boomers "have more chronic disease, more disability, and lower self-rated health than those of the previous generation."[45] Obesity, diabetes, hypertension, and heart disease are prevalent chronic conditions experienced by Baby Boomers. They also suffer from depression and addiction. There is a growing body of medical evidence that links diabetes to cognitive decline and perhaps even to Alzheimer's. In addition, the long-term effects of COVID are yet to be fully understood.

The CDC study went on to warn that that providing care can exacerbate chronic health conditions among caregivers. "Although providing informal care can bring many benefits, it is also a source of a chronic stress. Caregivers might experience this stress because of the physical demands of caregiving, the challenges of balancing work and other responsibilities with the caregiving role, the trouble with managing problematic behaviors of the people they care for, or the emotional difficulty of watching a loved one's health decline. Stress coping models have shown that the strain associated with caregiving can result in psychological distress and interference with the immune system and cardiovascular functions. Caregivers might also engage in health behaviors that contribute to negative health outcomes because of limited time to be physically active, attend medical appointments, or manage their own chronic conditions. Together, these physiological and behavioral changes increase the likelihood of developing new physical and mental health conditions."

As Baby Boomers age, my cohort will be less able to provide the informal care for the seniors who rely on us. In addition, my generation may need more care as we age due to the prevalence of chronic conditions. But who will care for us? The relative baby bust of Generation X will make it even more difficult to secure caregivers "In 2018, there were 7 potential family caregivers per 1 adult. By 2030, when all baby boomers will be aged 65 years or older, there will be only 4 potential family caregivers per 1 adult, increasing the burden on the caregiver workforce. The number of caregivers might not be sufficient to provide care for baby boomers when they need care."

During the last years of my mother's life, almost every weekend I made the four-hour, round-trip trek from the San Francisco Bay Area to Placerville in the foothills of the Sierras. I was fortunate in that I had a job with benefits. At first, I exhausted all my paid time off (PTO). That wasn't enough, though, to cover the time I had to take off to care for my mom, so I took a 10 percent pay cut to be allowed to take an extra one day off every two weeks. I was working for a Fortune 500 company in Silicon Valley, and the performance expectations were very high. In addition, my children were still reliant on me. While I escaped some of the more devasting physical conditions associated with chronic stress, I noticed a significant increase in my anxiety. For me, stress and anxiety exaggerated my fear of heights and bridges. To this day, I will go miles out of my way not to have to cross a bridge. Now that I have moved to the Portland, Oregon area that can sometimes be very hard to do.

DAUGHTERS

While I have one sibling, a brother, he was not involved in my mother's care. That is all too common. As I look across my extended family and friends, sons and brothers do not see caring for their elder relatives as a core responsibility. Most do not participate in care, although some provide a level of financial support. According to the Bureau of Labor Statistics, "more than 22 million American women spend more than three hours a day providing unpaid care for an elderly person."

This was certainly true for me. While I was actively caring for my mother at the end of her life, I took time off work, took a 10 percent cut in pay, dipped into savings, and paid out of pocket each month to cover expenses not covered by Social Security or other government programs I accessed on my mother's behalf. The 10 percent pay cut will impact my earnings calculation for my future Social Security payments. Did taking this time off impact my career? It is hard to say. What I can say is that I did not receive a promotion after taking this time off, and I was laid off eighteen months after my mother passed.

In total, I spent $25,000 to purchase a trailer for my mother to live in and to update it to accommodate her needs and make space for her knickknacks and other personal belonging—to, in effect, make it a home. I saw this decision as a trade-off between paying $3,000 out of pocket each month or more to subsidize my mother's stay in a board-and-care and making an investment in property that I could at some later point hope to sell and recoup. Even though it bit into my savings, it was the only practical alternative.

During the almost two years my mother lived in the trailer, each week I would purchase items at the grocery store not covered by food stamps—detergents, soap and shampoo, and cleaning products. I paid for her subscription for her medic alert bracelet that called a service should she have a fall or other emergency. I paid for her to go to the hairdresser and for all her clothes. I took her out to lunch at least once a week when she was able to go. As more and more of her Social Security check was needed for increased time with caregivers and medical co-pays, I paid the space rental fee for the trailer and for additional time with her paid caregivers.

I remember a few months after my mother's passing going through my checking account surprised to see a positive balance at the end of each month. I think I had a fair amount of denial about how much money I was actually spending on her care.

A study by AARP found that my experience is the norm for family members who care for elderly relatives: "Researchers surveyed nearly 2,000 family caregivers representing a variety of races and ethnicities in July and August 2016 and asked them to keep a diary of their expenditures. The study found that family caregivers spent an average of nearly $7,000 a year of their own money—more than

$7,400 in 2019 dollars. That spiked to nearly $12,000—$12,700 when adjusted for inflation—for caregivers who lived an hour or more from the care recipient. Costs generally were slightly higher if those receiving the care were 50 or older."[46]

Since I lived three hours from my mother, I estimate that the $12,000 cost was probably accurate. In addition to the direct expenses, I should also factor in transportation costs including gas and bridge tolls. I was fortunate in that when I needed to spend the night, my mother's neighbor had a large sleeping porch and generously let me stay with her, so I did not have to pay for a hotel room. In all, $12,000 a year for the three most intensive years of caregiving added up to a $36,000 hit to my savings and retirement fund.

The weekly expenses, almost while significant, went unnoticed as I went about doing what I needed to do to care for my mother. It was the big surprise expenses that really hit me. There were three, the largest of which was the funeral cost. My mother thought she had covered her funeral expenses by purchasing a plot in a cemetery in the Bay Area many years ago. However, that left more than $5,000 of uncovered expenses still, including the cost of the casket, the funeral home, transportation of the body, and cemetery fees. I was fortunate in that my cousins helped me with the reception costs. While a cremation would have been about a $1,000, my mother's strong religious beliefs would not allow for this option.

Another big surprise resulted from my mother's declining ability to manage her own finances and a huge unpaid bill to her caregiver. Having been a CPA, my mother prided herself on her ability to manage her own finances. She was very reluctant to allow me access to her checkbook. Over time, as her health declined, we would have a monthly check writing session where I sat with her and drafted the checks for her signature. It was only then that I saw that my mother's spending was far exceeding her income. Ultimately, I finally convinced her to give me her check book so I could better help her manage her budget.

Except for extreme cases in which a conservatorship can be granted, seniors are free to make their own financial decisions and their own mistakes, even though the elderly may be making imprudent financial decisions. As family caregivers, we can only advise and try our best to influence. Without a power of attorney, I did not even legally have visibility into my mother's accounts. When I finally convinced her that she needed my help, it was too late. Her caregiver had not been paid for over a month, even while she had been making multiple charitable donations. I had a $1,000 bill to pay.

Medical bills were the last big area of surprise. Even though my mother had Medicare and a Medigap insurance policy with good coverage, there were gaps. Diapers were a large, uncovered expense, as were expenses for hearing aids, dental visits, prescription glasses, and ambulance co-pays. Each time my mother fell and pushed the button, the service dispatched an ambulance, resulting in a $250 co-pay. The last week before my mother entered skilled nursing, she pushed the button three times. In the above-mentioned AARP study, medical expenses made up 25 percent of the costs borne by family members for the senior in their care.

As a female and a member of the Baby Boom generation, I am very typical of those who care for our seniors. The physical and financial toll it took on me is also, unfortunately, very representative. I did what I did to satisfy my own code of ethics and sense of familial responsibility. I believe that my mother benefited greatly from my help. While my mother ultimately spent the last ten months of her life in a skilled nursing home, my support enabled her to live independently until she was 93. The impact on her and on society at large for the thousands of seniors who stay at home cared for by their daughters is immense.

According to the Stanford Encyclopedia of Philosophy, "One can argue that since the human care involved in taking care of children and elders creates a public good, it should clearly be characterized as work, and those who are caretakers, primarily women, should be fairly compensated for it by society or the state." Instead, a caregiver's labor is either unpaid or underpaid, justified in the name of personal and familial responsibility. Caretakers have limited power to direct the finances of those they are responsible for and no power to ensure that each family member bears an equal responsibility for taking care of their parent, women are expected to shoulder the responsibility of caring for our seniors.

Again and again, daughters, like me, are the ones who do this work. In fact, the unpaid labor of women caring for seniors is saving society billions! Shurtz, and others, estimate, "The impact of unpaid family care is profound on the care-receiver and the care giver. Long-term care is mostly provided through freely given and loving labor. It often allows the care-receiver to remain at home with quality care, avoid the devastating costs of institutional care and personal financial ruin, and save taxpayer billions of dollars. The estimated "the value of replacing family caregivers with professional paid caregivers is over $500 billion annually."[47]

LOW-WAGE CARE GIVERS

Let's return to the example of California, mentioned earlier. In California home health care aides are mostly women; more than half are women of color. Immigrants make up one-quarter of the workforce. One in five home care workers is a single mother. The average salary in 2022 was $29,518 according to salary.com. One in four live in households below the federal poverty line, and over half live in households under 200 percent of the federal poverty line. The rate of workers without health coverage—more than one in three—is considerably higher than the general population, while the rate of employer-provided insurance is considerably lower.[48]

These women, making poverty level wages, are entrusted to care for our most vulnerable seniors. The job is innately a very stressful one as caregivers perform the most intimate tasks—bathing, transferring and cleaning the feces, blood and urine of the seniors in their charge. In addition to the physical stressors, caregivers deal with the emotional challenges of taking care of seniors who may be battling depression and dementia.

Many home health aides are victims of abuse and even violence in the workplace. Workplace aggression, or threatening behavior, were reported by 7 to 16 percent. Approximately 30 percent of homecare workers reported being sexually harassed. Workplace violence or physical assaults were reported by between 2 -to 11 percent of homecare workers.[49] Since it is common for violence against women to be under-reported, it's likely that these statistics are a low estimate of what occurs in the privacy of a home environment, where a home health aide is alone with their charge or another family member who is also their employer.

In addition to the physical stresses of the job, home health aides experience emotional and psychological stress. These stresses can come from the unique challenges of managing both the boredom and unpredictability of the seniors in their care, but also from the terms of employment that are common among low wage workers—lack of a fixed schedule, variation in work hours impacting wages, lack of insurance, need to work while sick or if a family member is sick, struggles with transportation. For live in caregivers, the death or removal of the senior to a care facility could jeopardize their housing.

There are two principal employers of paid caregivers—private agencies and local government (a complicated and often disjointed web of services that we'll explore in depth in the next chapter). Caregivers can also be self-employed. Like other self-employed workers, there are now online brokers that intermediate between workers seeking employment and families needing care. Private agencies and online brokers make money by charging an uplift to the wages earned by the caregivers. For example, at one point my mother employed caregivers who worked for a large agency. The caregivers were paid about twelve dollars and hour, and the agency charged my mother twenty-two dollars an hour. Caregivers who worked for the agency full-time did receive insurance coverage, but shift variations sometimes made this difficult to secure.

The turnover rate is very high among caregivers employed by private agencies. Home Care Pulse data shows that though the typical home care agency keeps its caregivers for around fifteen months, many only retain their workers for half a year or less. My mother experienced first-hand the high turnover rate and job dissatisfaction with agency-employed caregivers, that can be as high as 67 percent on a yearly basis, according to some estimates.

Many caregivers are self-employed. Private individuals can be retained to provide most of the same services with fees that are 20 percent to 30 percent lower. However, independent caregivers are typically uninsured, do not go through background checks and may be unable to provide alternatives in case they are not available to work on short notice." My mother employed caregivers who were self-employed when she lived in independent living and in the trailer. The wages varied over time from $18 to $24 per hour.

I found that the self-employed caregivers delivered the highest quality of care. These women, and they were all women, created their own networks to ensure coverage if someone had to miss work or was too ill. In the San Francisco Bay Area, the caregiver networks were organized by cultural groups—Filipinos, Salvadorans and South Pacific Islanders had their networks. In Placerville, the networks were based on family relationships. A mother and aunt team cared for my mother at the end of her life. While $24 per hour seems high, the caregivers only worked for my mother a maximum of four hours per day. They made additional income with other clients and work hours could vary greatly. There was no paid time off and caregivers would come to work with colds or back injuries to keep their checks coming in. I still keep in touch with my mother's former caregivers. With COVID, both have lost clients and work hours.

COVID'S IMPACT AND THE FUTURE

The coming crisis in Senior care has been put into bold relief with COVID. Virtual prisoners in their rooms, residents in long term care facilities experienced months and months of isolation and many lost their lives to the virus. The short comings of institutional living were front page news. The challenges brought about by COVID were not new. The limitations of institutional living brought about by has long been apparent to those struggling to care for their parents. The political horse trading needed to pass Medicare left many senior programs subject to state level requirements and funding cuts.

Caregivers are the key to enabling seniors to live at home and in their communities. Today, the responsibility for providing care for the elderly falls overwhelmingly to women, wives and daughters who are stepping up to the responsibility, even when their own health and financial security may be jeopardized. With the aging of the Baby Boomer generation, the burden on caregivers continues to grow, with a limited outlook for relief. Baby Boomers are less healthy than the Greatest Generation of my mother's era. Baby Boomers have higher incidences of chronic diseases which may result in more assistance needed with the ADLs as we age. Female Baby Boomers live longer with chronic illnesses and are more likely to need care for a longer period of time.

While we are caring for our parents, it is not clear who will care for us. Gen X is a relative baby bust leaving far fewer family members to provide care. For many of us, the responsibility of providing care for our own parents has left us poorer and sicker as we age.

Our dependence on low wage paid caregivers is not equitable nor sustainable. Home health care workers left the occupation in droves due to COVID. Fear of exposure to COVID due to a lack of PPE and training, low wages and, for those who stayed, long hours contributed to a serious shortage of home health workers across the country leaving many elderly and disabled without care. The COVID crisis has been a tipping point of sorts to draw attention to the long festering problem of the lack of adequate wages and working conditions for home health aides.

According to a recent *New York Times* report: "The Bureau of Labor Statistics estimated job losses of 342,000 in the direct care work force in 2020— including nursing home and other residential care and home care staff. (Typically, employment in these categories rises each year.) The losses came either through layoffs or from people resigning because of health problems or fears related to Covid, lack of childcare and other impediments. The labor force has rebounded somewhat in 2021, however, "more than 800,000 older and disabled people who qualify for Medicaid are on state waiting lists for home care. Agencies serving private-pay clients are turning away business. Congregate living looks less attractive after Covid, as residents died, and family members were locked out for months. Moreover, a return to workplaces means that some adult children can no longer provide elder care. Even before the pandemic, the Bureau of Labor Statistics projected the addition of one million home care jobs by 2029."[50]

As home health workers look to negotiate higher wages in light of the current labor shortage, middle class families struggle to figure out how to pay for what was already a significant cost for which there is no government program or subsidy or even a meaningful tax break. Even in the face of this serious problem impacting many families across the county, there is little appetite in Congress to pass the elements of the Build Back Better plan which could have a positive impact. Biden's plan would have expanded Medicaid funding for home healthcare aides and implemented a $5,000 annual tax deduction to partially offset out of pocket costs for family health care providers. However, even these modest proposals could not find support in Congress.

There are solutions, albeit not a comprehensive plan that the dependent elderly and their caregivers want and deserve. In the next chapter, we will look at the patchwork quilt of programs which counties and states administer to assist families in caring for their dependent loved ones. In the chapter to follow, we look at a range of solutions for families focusing on how to address the biggest challenges, housing and healthcare. We look at how evolving technology can play a role in keeping seniors safely living at home in their communities.

As families, wives, and daughters we do what we can to provide for our elderly dependents. History has taught us that for things to change we need to move outside of the private sphere and advocate for legal and public policy changes to provide a safer and more equitable system for the provision of care.

CHAPTER FOUR

A PATCHWORK QUILT

U nlike the all-encompassing, large-scale enterprises of institutional living, the supports that allow seniors to safely age in place are fragmented and localized. As we saw in chapter two, the compromise that was forged to gain support from Southern Democrats for Medicare passage resulted in Medicaid and other human services programs being implemented at the state level, where they are subject to state-imposed requirements and frequent budget cuts. Long waiting lists for senior housing, Medicaid beds in nursing homes, and in-home support services are commonplace. In addition, there is little coordination between programs, so seniors have to apply at different offices and navigate different eligibility criteria to secure services. The system is not set up to seamlessly support seniors to safely live at home or to support the families and caregivers who care for them.

As we learned last chapter, Mary employed caregivers through a large national agency and as independent contractors. In looking to secure caregiver support for my mother, we applied to the county's In-Home Supportive Services (IHSS) program, but the share-of-cost eligibility requirements precluded her from getting the help she needed. Hospice was another program that provided some level of support but left important gaps. During this time, I consistently stepped up my level of caretaking and support, ultimately reducing my hours at work so I could care for my mother.

In this chapter, we'll explore the patchwork of programs that supports seniors to live safely at home, including Meals on Wheels, SNAP, Senior Day Care, HEAP, and other state-run programs.

IHSS (IN HOME SUPPORTIVE SERVICES)

In the last chapter, we learned about the network of self-employed and private agency employed caregivers who my mother relied on.

At the county-level, states also employ caregivers for Medicaid-eligible seniors who demonstrate a need for help with the Activities of Daily Living through the IHSS (In-Home Supportive Services Program). In 2017 and 2018, my mother needed care in El Dorado County, the county IHSS workers were getting paid $10.40 per hour. IHSS workers had to pay $50 to be fingerprinted and complete a training program for which they were not paid. IHSS pays for individuals, including family members, to act as caregivers. In their 2016 annual report, El Dorado County noted that "Care providers who are family members (immediate and non-immediate) make up 65% of the total providers. Non-Family care providers make-up 35% of the providers and consist of friends, neighbors, and persons hired from the Registry. The majority of care providers are women, i.e. mothers, wives, and daughters."[51]

IHSS can be a lifeline for low-income seniors and other individuals with disabilities, enabling them to live at home or in the community instead of in an institution. One of the drivers behind funding for IHSS is the cost savings afforded to states and counties from keeping the disabled out of nursing homes. However, the funding mix for IHSS is not the same as the funding mix for nursing homes. The reliance on a greater mix of state and county funds leaves IHSS vulnerable to budget cuts in times of recession. States and county governments cannot print money like the federal government, so social service program budgets that are reliant on these fund sources are at risk. In California, IHHS is funded by a combination of state, county, and federal Medicaid funds.

According to the 2022-23 California state budget: "Overall, the effective federal reimbursement rate for IHSS is about 54 percent. The remaining nonfederal share of IHSS costs is covered by the state and counties." And the state's in-home supportive services brochure states, "In 2017, the amount counties were to contribute to the IHSS program collectively increased by about $600 million. However, the vehicle fees and sales taxes that counties rely on to pay their contributions have not provided sufficient revenue to cover these increases."

In contrast, with the passage of the Affordable Care Act (ACA), the federal government pays a higher share of Medicaid costs, which is the primary source of funding for nursing home patients. "The federal share of Medicaid is determined by a formula set in statute that is based on a state's per capita income. The formula is designed so that the federal government pays a larger share of program costs in poorer states. The federal share (FMAP) varies by state from a floor of 50 percent to a high of 77 percent in 2020."[52] So from the perspective of State and County administrators, it is more cost effective to place seniors in nursing homes instead of providing in-home supportive services even though the true cost of nursing home care is much higher.

The requirement that states balance their budgets creates a no-win situation for seniors and caregivers. The dynamics of the California State budget highlights the tension created between the growing need to provide care for an ever-increasing population of seniors with disabilities and paying home health aides a living wage. To attempt to square the circle, California embarked on a trial program in 2012 called the Coordinated Care Initiative. The State billed the program as a cost-savings initiative with the state realizing reduced costs while providing better care for IHSS participants. Cost savings were to be realized by coordinating care across healthcare providers and multiple State programs. The budget analysis from the California governor's office showed that the program was successful in removing the burden of costs from county government but, since the goal was to reduce costs to the state, the program had to be discontinued since the state's budget reduction goal was not met.

The 2017-2018 State IHSS Budget Analysis summarized the reason for the termination of the program: "Since the IHSS county MOE was instituted, the General Fund has borne a disproportionate amount of growing IHSS program costs, growing at an average rate of 20 percent annually, from $1.7 billion in 2012-13 to an estimated $3.5 billion in 2016-17. County IHSS program costs, by contrast, have increased at an average rate of around 4 percent annually over the same period."

State law contains a poison pill provision that automatically discontinues the pilot program if the Director of Finance determines that the CCI does not generate annual net General Fund savings and is therefore not cost-effective. The Governor's budget reflects a determination that the CCI is not cost-effective, which the administration primarily attributes to growing General Fund costs under the IHSS county MOE. As a result, the IHSS county MOE will end on July 1, 2017, and be replaced with the prior IHSS program cost-sharing ratio of counties paying 35 percent of nonfederal program costs and the state paying the remaining 65 percent."[53]

Talk about a poison pill indeed. Counties are already bracing for the impact. San Bernardino County, the fifth-most populous county in California and fourteenth-most populous in the U.S., has warned that its IHHS costs could rise to $160 million in fiscal year 2021-22.[54]

The funding model for IHSS pits the needs of counties against the state, seniors against other groups requiring Social Services, and care givers against those that they care for. It is important to remember that the average cost for an IHSS program recipient is $12,000, while the cost for a Medicaid bed in a skilled nursing facility is six to ten times more. The problem is that cost savings is impossible to realize while the funding mix for IHSS contains a large share of cost from State and local governments and the population needing in-home support services is increasing. In addition, recent lawsuits have awarded care givers higher wages, pay for travel time and time spent waiting for medical appointments, and over time. The lower level of federal funding for IHSS leaves everyone scrambling to secure a section of a shrinking pie.

Keep in mind that even before this budget crisis, cost-cutting measures kept IHSS services to a minimum for those who qualified. When a potential IHSS recipient applies for the program at a county office, the determination of their eligibility is a two-step process that takes into account the applicant's income and need for services.

IHSS Application Process

Once a county worker verifies that an individual is financially eligible for IHSS, a county social worker visits the home of the recipient to determine whether there is a need for services. To perform this assessment, the social worker uses a uniform assessment tool to determine the number of hours for each type of IHSS service for which a recipient qualifies in order to remain safely in their own home. Figure 1 provides a list of the types of services an IHSS recipient may be eligible to receive.[55]

FIGURE 1: EXAMPLES OF SERVICES AVAILABLE
TO IN-HOME SUPPORTIVE SERVICES RECIPIENTS

Tasks	Examples
Domestic Services	Cleaning, dusting, picking up, changing linens, changing light bulbs, wheelchair maintenance, and taking out garbage.
Laundry	Sorting, washing, hanging, folding, mending, and ironing.
Shopping and Errands	Purchasing groceries and putting them away, picking up prescriptions, and buying clothing.
Meal Preparation	Planning menus, preparing food, and setting the table.
Meal Cleanup	Washing dishes and putting them away.
Feeding	Feeding.
Ambulation	Assisting recipient with walking or moving in home or to car.
Bathing, Oral Hygiene, Grooming	Bathing recipient, getting in or out of the shower, hair care, shaving, and grooming.
Routine Bed Baths	Sponge bathing the body.
Dressing	Putting on/taking off clothing.
Medications and Assistance with Prosthetic Devices	Medication administration assistance; taking off/ putting on, maintaining, and cleaning prosthetic devices.
Bowel and Bladder	Bedpan/ bedside commode care, application of diapers, assisting with getting on/off commode or toilet.
Menstrual Care	External application of sanitary napkins.
Transfer	Assistance with standing/ sitting.
Repositioning/ Rubbing Skin	Circulation promotion and skin care.
Respiration	Assistance with oxygen and oxygen equipment.
Protective Supervision	Ensuring recipient is not harming themselves.

The uniform assessment tool, known as the hourly task guidelines (HTGs), assists the social worker in ranking the recipient's impairment level on a five–point scale known as the functional index (FI) ranking.

Figure 2 shows each of the potential FI rankings that may be assessed by a social worker, and what they mean for the impairment level of the recipient. Each FI ranking corresponds to an established range of service hours for a particular task. For example, a recipient who receives an FI ranking of 2 on the "feeding" task may be authorized to receive between 0.7 hours and 2.3 hours of feeding per week. The corresponding range of hours varies depending on the particular task being assessed. For example, meal preparation services range from three to seven hours. Also, if an individual is assessed as having an FI ranking of 1 for any given task, he or she will not receive any authorized hours for that task.

FIGURE 2: FUNCTIONAL INDEX RATING SCALE

Functional Index	Impairment Implications
1	Able to perform function without human assistance—independent.
2	Able to perform a function, but needs verbal assistance (reminding, encouraging).
3	Able to perform a function with some human, physical assistance.
4	Able to perform a function with substantial human assistance.
5	Cannot perform the function with or without human assistance.

Assignment of Hours

Once a social worker has determined the number of hours to authorize for a recipient, the recipient is notified of the number of hours they have been authorized for each task. Using the HTGs, social workers may authorize between one and 283 total hours per month of IHSS services. Currently, recipients receive an average of about 85 hours of IHSS per month. Recipients who receive over 195 hours of service each month are considered to be severely impaired.

Most program participants receive about 20 hours of care per week. This model is far short of full-time care and provides little flexibility to increase hours if a client gets sick, is recovering from a fall, or experiences other spike in need.

The following narrative of a disabled woman applying for services illustrates the gap between the need and what IHSS provides:

> My own experience starkly illustrates the struggles a person with a severe disability has in getting needed services. Before applying for IHSS, I researched the program extensively, studying how they determine needs and decide how many hours applicants receive. As my needs are significant, I documented in detail how much time I required for each task, including explanations of why my most personal needs—dressing, bathing, using the toilet—take the time they do. Yet that was not enough. Despite the several pages of detailed information I gave her, my first social worker seemed to already have a set number of hours in her mind when she arrived at my home to evaluate me. She out-and-out said that I wouldn't get as many hours as I "wanted"—as if any person would want more care than they actually needed—and made it evident that she would disregard my documentation, while also claiming to be impressed by it. When I received my "Notice of Action," I found that she had given me only 180 hours per month, 100 less than the IHSS maximum of 283 that I required."[56]

This applicant's experience mirrors that of my mother when we applied for IHSS in El Dorado County.

Although my mother was eligible for Medicaid and food stamps, the IHSS-eligibility calculation resulted in her needing to pay a significant share of cost toward receiving services. Share-of-costs calculations take into account the applicant's income and medical expenses. Given my mother's Social Security income of $1,700 she had to document a $500-per-month share of cost. The wages she paid to her caregivers weren't calculated at the actual rate of pay, but at the payrate the county provided caregivers, which was about half of what we were actually paying. Without the ability to include all of her actual expenses, my mother did not qualify for a full subsidy.

In addition, the needs assessment showed that she could receive less than 20 hours of care based on her stated ability to perform daily tasks. The caregiver would be a new person, chosen from a registry service. Ultimately, we determined that the program was not a good fit for my mother's needs.

The frustrating truth was my mother required in-home care services- to continue to live independently, but the program's limitations precluded her from participating. We continued to pay private caregivers, which ultimately exhausted her financial resources and left her with too little care hours to meet her increasing needs.

The elderly and disabled who participate in IHSS can face other negative outcomes as well. Many program participants live with a level of care below what they need to meet their daily needs, leaving them isolated and vulnerable, especially when there is a spike in their care needs following an illness or injury. At worst, IHSS participants may fall victims to the very people employed to care for them. The disabled woman who recounted her story applying for services was robbed by a former caregiver. She aptly pointed out the risk of having low-wage workers with limited training having access to the homes of vulnerable patients. Far more screening, training and oversight would help to ensure safety for seniors and support wage increases for caregivers.

The idea behind IHSS is a good one, allowing the elderly and disabled to live at home in their community cared for by relatives and professional care providers who are paid for their services. The reality of the program leaves much to be desired. State and local funding models leave the program vulnerable to budget cuts which result in waiting lists for services and cuts to service hours for existing clients. The income threshold to qualify for services is very low, leaving many seniors without access to the program. Seniors may need in home care, but have too much income to qualify for IHSS, but too little income to pay market rate for the level of care needed. Caregivers are not paid a living wage and may lack the training needed to be effective. Understandably the turnover rate is very high. Even given all of these programmatic limitations, the need for this program is growing dramatically as the Baby Boom generation ages and requires in home health services.

SSI (SUPPLEMENTAL SECURITY INCOME)

After navigating the process for IHSS and finding out that the program did not fit for my mother, I did not apply for SSI on her behalf. SSI is a program run by the Social Security administration to provide payments to very low-income seniors aged 65 and older. A single person can have no more than $2,000 in liquid assets; couples may not have more than $3,000. Unlike eligibility for food stamps and other social programs, vehicles are counted as assets for the purpose of SSI eligibility. So is land, cash, insurance, and anything that can be liquidated for cash is counted.

There is also a strict income test for SSI eligibility. The income limit for SSI is less than $800; however, the income calculation is complex, so to determine eligibility seniors should visit the Social Security website. For instance, food stamps and heating assistance payments are not counted for the purpose of calculating income. With a Social Security benefit of $1,700 per month, my mother was well over the limit for included individual income. Any payments I made on her behalf for food and shelter, and any in-kind provisions, would also have been counted.

Even with these stringent requirements, 7.8 million Americans currently receive SSI benefits, which cap out at $794 per month. SSI acts as a backstop for the poorest of seniors and the disabled who may not have Social Security or other sources of income. With the low payment rate, seniors reliant on SSI are condemned to living in poverty. "Decades of Congressional neglect mean that SSI—a critical program that should be protecting people from poverty—now instead traps disabled people and seniors in deep and enduring poverty when it's supposed to be giving them a lifeline out of it," says Rebecca Vallas, a senior fellow at The Century Foundation.[57]

A PATCHWORK QUILT

In addition to Medicare, Medicaid and IHSS, there is a veritable patchwork quilt of programs to support the elderly to secure food, obtain discounted heat, electricity and telephone service, upgrade their homes, get transportation to medical appointments, and have a safe environment to spend the day—Senior Day Care.

Like IHSS, these programs are administered at the state and local level. Access to these programs is not uniform from county to county and state to state. Many may have waiting lists, and all have some form of eligibility criteria. Each program must be accessed independently. There is no one-stop shop or uniform application process.

Ferreting out each of these programs was an effort in detective work. It required that I complete a mountain of paperwork, transport my mother to various eligibility interviews, and track the provision of services. My mother and I were relatively fortunate in that we are persistent, educated, have citizenship status, and have access to key documents and financial records. The El Dorado County Senior Center in Placerville was a helpful resource where I picked up pamphlets, asked questions, and secured resources on behalf of my mother. However, I was my mother's case manager, putting together a changing patchwork of services to keep my mother in her home.

My mother's specific patchwork of services included Meals on Wheels, SNAP (Food Stamps), HEAP (Subsidized heating), Life-Line (subsidized telephone landline), Hospice, and Senior Day Care. Not all of these programs ultimately proved successful for my mother. In addition, where costs were concerned, even if my mother qualified, the most programs offered was a discount or subsidy, leaving a bill at the end of the day. I will share the experience we had with these programs, and encourage seniors and those who care for seniors, to research available programs in your area.

MEALS ON WHEELS

Meals on Wheels in a nation-wide program which is administered at the local level by a small staff and a cadre of volunteers. In Placerville, the Meals on Wheels program delivered a fresh meal or one which could be re-heated on or around the noon hour Monday through Friday. Meals were not delivered on weekends or holidays. To be eligible for Meals on Wheels, a senior must be at least 60 years old and homebound—unable to shop, prepare meals or attend a congregant lunch site. In some areas, referral from a doctor or social worker is required. In Placerville, Meals on Wheels charged my mother $3 for the home delivered lunch and this was a suggested price. If she was not able to pay, she would not be turned away from the service.

More than 70 percent of the annual budget for Meals on Wheels comes from contributions from the community. Meals on Wheels receives some federal support through Older American Act and Medicaid dollars, as well as from the USDA. In Placerville, all of the people who deliver the meals are volunteers. The federal fund source also provided for the local Senior Center to host in-person lunches once a week. The meal was prepared at the same kitchen as Meals on Wheels but served at the Elks Lodge and the Senior Center. Unfortunately, these lunches were cancelled due to COVID.

Across the United States, each year 2.4 million seniors are served by Meals on Wheels.[58] I understand that my mother was fortunate in that in many areas there is a waiting list for Meals on Wheels. According to Meals on Wheels, "83% of low-income and food insecure seniors do not receive meals they may benefit from, due in part to insufficient funding."[59] In some areas, the service can charge much more. With COVID, some local programs have changed their delivery service, dropping off a week's-worth of frozen meals in one delivery with the expectation that they be defrosted and reheated. In addition to a healthy meal including a salad, entrée, starch, vegetable, bread, dessert, and milk, a significant benefit of the program is the companionship provided by the volunteers. Every day, a smiling face would provide another touch for my mother. Someone to make sure she was okay and to spend a minute chatting about the day. COVID has robbed the program of that element.

While I was a big fan of Meals on Wheels; my mother was not. She did not like the food and could not abide by the idea that she would throw away the part of the meal she did not like and eat the rest. We made three attempts to keep up the program, and finally the local administrator said that my mother had refused the food too many times to continue enrollment. Her slot would be given to someone else.

Ultimately, what I wanted for my mother was for her to be able to eat healthy meals to help her manage her diabetes. If she was skipping meals because she did not like the food, Meals on Wheels was not a solution. What worked better for my mother was SNAP (Supplemental Nutrition Assistance Program) commonly known as food stamps.

SNAP/CALFRESH

Sadly, food stamps carry a lot of negative associations. It was a heavy lift to get my mother to apply. But once we were over the hump, we found that SNAP, or CalFresh as it is known in California, was the best way to ensure she received support to buy food she would actually eat to help get her diabetes under control. While stereotypes abound about SNAP recipients, nationwide one in ten senior households rely on food stamps.[60] In addition, according to the National Council on Aging, in 2021, three out of five seniors who could qualify for SNAP do not receive the benefit. This represents more than five million people.[61]

Barriers to participation include lack of awareness about the program and an impression that the benefit level is too low to make the application process worthwhile. The CalFresh application I completed on my mother's behalf was on-line. It was a simple initial screening, but many seniors lack access to the internet or struggle with navigating on-line forms. Following the initial screening, I helped my mother gather key documents for an in-person meeting with the County eligibility worker. I had to produce my mother's bank statements, the Social Security award letter, and birth certificate. Eligibility needed to be validated every six months. Eligibility requirements for food stamps vary from county to county, and verification of income and assets is required.

To be eligible for CalFresh in El Dorado County in 2017, my mother could have no more than $2,000 in assets. This did not count a home or a car. There was also an income eligibility threshold. With my mother's Social Security income of $1,700 per month she qualified. Income calculations include Social Security, but deductions are taken for medical expenses and shelter costs. There was no work requirement or time limit for benefits since my mother was over 90 years old and disabled.

Food stamps are not actual stamps. My mother received a debit card or EBT card, that can be used at local grocery stores to purchase food items. As her authorized delegate, I received a card as well so I could shop on her behalf. At the check-out register, I entered the card into the card reader and chose EBT. The checkout system automatically identifies the purchases which are eligible under the program and debits the card. If there is a balance, you can pay with another debit or credit card or with cash. The system also tracks the balance on the card for the month. Each month my mother received $197.

You cannot purchase cleaning products, grooming products, toilet paper, diapers, or hot to-go items with food stamps. My mother was a big fan of the Safeway grilled chicken from the deli counter. She could not buy the chicken hot with her EBT card but could get the same chicken cold from the refrigerator case next to the deli counter. EBT was a godsend for my mother. She could choose fresh fruit including fruit cups without sugar, and packaged fruit from the deli counter. She loved the deli coleslaw, pasta salads and bagged salads as well. We would buy pasta and tomato sauce for her home health aide to cook and fresh fish with pre-chopped vegetables. I frequently lost the battle in the ice cream aisle since my mother was a big fan of its ice cream sandwich cookies.

In the year plus that my mother lived in the trailer and received food stamps, her dependence on insulin dropped dramatically. I attribute this at least in part to the healthy food she was able to access through CalFresh. The $197 per month covered almost all of her food purchases, since her meal portions were quite small. This boost to her income allowed the rest of her Social Security check to be spent on medical expenses, including insurance, co-pays, medicine, and home health care. My mother's experience was validated by a study by the National Council on Aging: " A recent study of 60,000 low-income Maryland seniors found that SNAP participants are 23% less likely to enter a nursing home and 4% less likely to be hospitalized in the year after receiving SNAP than non-participants. SNAP participation was also linked to lower overall health care expenditures and Medicaid/Medicare costs."[62]

In addition to the ability to access appetizing and healthy food to manage her diabetes and free up money to pay for additional time with her home health aide, the biggest benefit of SNAP participation was that it unlocked access to other benefits. As a recipient of food stamps, eligibility was almost automatic for other programs, including Lifeline and HEAP.

LIFELINE AND HEAP

LifeLine is a federal program administered at the state level through telecom providers to offer discounted landline and cell phone service to low-income residents. As a SNAP recipient, my mother automatically qualified for LifeLine. The regulations vary from state to state, but in California my mother was able to get landline service for approximately $25 per month. This included unlimited local calls and a limited number of long-distance domestic calls. My mother never learned to use a cell phone or the internet, but SNAP eligibility also unlocks eligibility for discounted cell phone and internet service as well as the purchase of cell phones. In 2005, under the Bush presidency, the FCC expanded the LifeLine program to include cell phones and internet service. An entire industry has grown up around this expansion.

The Low Income Home Energy Assistance Program (LIHEAP) assists eligible low-income households with their heating and cooling energy costs, bill payment assistance, energy crisis assistance, weatherization and energy-related home repairs. As a SNAP recipient, my mother was automatically eligible for the program which provided either a one-time payment of $500 to subsidize a propane delivery or a percentage decrease in her monthly electrical bill. My mother chose the monthly subsidy of approximately $40, which was deducted from her space rent since the park managed the utility bills for residents.

The HEAP program also includes a weatherization component. Weatherization improvements can be made to windows, heaters, air conditioners and water heaters. In California, energy efficiency and water conservation are goals of the program, in addition to improving the lives of the recipients. The HEAP program also offers low energy lightbulbs, low-flow shower heads, and power strips.

SNAP, LifeLine, and HEAP are federal programs administered at the state and local level. Program eligibility guidelines are subject to local regulations. Individual applications are required for each program, and, although validation is simplified by SNAP eligibility, additional verification is required. For HEAP, I needed to submit copies of prior energy bills for my mother. While applying on-line can initiate the process, I needed to print forms, secure my mother's signature and mail or fax forms back to the funding agency. HEAP required an in-person interview.

Federally funded programs are subject to the pendulum swings of expansion and contraction based on the vagaries of national politics. SNAP, for instance, is a frequent political hot potato. In March 2020, a federal judge has issued an injunction blocking the Trump administration from adopting a rule change that would have forced nearly 700,000 Americans off food stamps. The proposed rule change also would have mandated work requirements during the COVID emergency.[63]

The Biden administration reversed course under COVID, and then made the increase permanent in August 2021. Food stamp recipients saw a 25 percent increase in food stamp benefits, the largest jump in the history of the program. This was possible because Congressional approval was not required since the increase was based on a recalculation of the underlying nutritional standards which provide the basis for the per family calculations. However, some red states had already moved to cut off COVID enhanced SNAP benefits and institute work requirements.

The LifeLine program has also been subject to a culling of recipients following a GAO audit. With eligibility determination delegated to local telecom providers a GAO audit in 2017 found that eligibility could not be validated for a third of participants. In 2016, under Democratic oversight, the FCC looked to automate eligibility, linking to state HHS databases in the hope of ensuring that applicants who met qualifying income guidelines were enrolled in assistance. However, the implementation beginning in 2018 saw a dramatic drop in program enrollment. The planned linkages to state databases did not operate as designed requiring that thousands of participants re-apply for services.[64]

HEAP has its own set of challenges due to limited funding and eligibility hurdles. In addition, since the providers of weatherization services must necessarily come on site, seniors could be left vulnerable to scams and criminals who victimize them instead of providing services. However, the vast majority of HEAP contractors are honest, and seniors greatly benefit from the reduced energy costs and the comforts of new windows and updated heating and cooling systems.

HOSPICE

Hospice is not a place. It is a service. Toward the end of her residence in the little trailer, my mother's doctor deemed her eligible for hospice. His determination was based on an assessment of how long she had to live and her growing need for additional care. Typically, hospice services are reserved for patients in the last six months of their lives. As a hospice patient, my mother would no longer be in the cycle of falling, calling 911, transport to the ER, and release.

The role of hospice is to send a hospice nurse to provide regular check ins and to be available in case of emergency. The hope is to eliminate or at least reduce the need for emergency care with the regular visits and to allow my mother to stay in her home until she passed. Hospice does not provide round the clock care even for patients with extreme medical needs. The hospice nurse made it clear that at the very end of her life, I would need to be with my mother around the clock for weeks.

Both my mother and I appreciated the regular check ins from the hospice nurse, but in the event of a fall or other emergency, my mother was more comfortable calling 911 even though the Emergency room could do little but ensure that she was not concussed and to monitor her blood sugar. Since my mother was a hospice patient, these visits to the ER would necessitate a release from hospice before admittance. Hospice and hospital care cannot co-exist for a patient. Hospice is funded through Medicare and Medicaid.

Since hospice could not provide additional hours of home health care nor was it an option for my mother in case of emergency, ultimately, we opted out of hospice while my mother was living in the trailer. Hospice did, however, serve my mother when she was residing in Skilled nursing. In addition to the medical and care staff of the nursing home, visits from the hospice nurse provided me and my mother another insight into her health. The hospice nurse was especially helpful in encouraging my mother to participate in activities. She also was an effective lobbyist ensuring that my mother got her TV fixed and a room change when requested. My mother outlived the six-month timeline for hospice! On her 94th birthday, she was officially released from hospice care.

SENIOR DAY CARE

The final service in the patchwork quilt supporting my mother in staying in her home was Senior Day Care. Senior Day Care provides supervised activities, meals, and health services to participating seniors during the week. In Placerville, the Senior Day program operated out of the Senior Center.

My mother needed to arrange for transportation to get to the center and back home. Once there, the program provided a full complement of activities and a daily lunch meal. The Center was staffed to provide medication management including supervising insulin injections. At the Placerville site, there was also a shower facility and staff would assist seniors in getting a shower during the day if needed. There was also a restful nap room with peaceful music and comfy recliners.

I accompanied my mother to two trips to the Senior Day program, but ultimately, she chose not to participate. The cost of a day at the program was $58 per day. At the time of application, I had not yet applied for Medicaid for my mother. Had I done so, the cost would have been reduced if a Medicaid slot was available. Generally, most adult day care is covered under Medicaid waivers that take into account an applicant's income, financial resources, and functional ability. In 2019, most waivers limited a participant's monthly income to $2,313, and Medicaid-covered slots can be limited in some senior day care programs.[65]

The plan was not to replace her home health care providers, but to provide a change of pace one to two days per week. My mother was worried about getting in and out of her caregiver's truck to get to the center. She also felt that she would not relate to the other participants since many had early onset dementia. I had hoped that she would ultimately choose to participate since the advantage of having a change to her routine, including the opportunity to hear live music or watch travelogues would be something she would enjoy. Like with Meals on Wheels, even though I thought that participation would benefit my mother, ultimately it was her choice to participate.

WRAP UP

I tried my best to keep my mother living in a home environment for as long as possible. With some success I navigated the patchwork quilt of government programs available to help seniors to live at home. Fortunately, rural California had a robust social safety net relative to other states. I did not encounter long waiting lists but did have to navigate complex application processes and found that IHSS and hospice were too limited to meet my mother's needs. With her dwindling resources, programs like CalFresh (food stamps), HEAP, and LifeLine extended her budget enough to make independent living work.

Eligibility for government programs was an option for my mother only when she had exhausted all of her savings and her sole remaining source of income was Social Security. For most middle-class Americans there is no government support to age comfortably at home. Medicare does not pay for in-home support outside of a limited visits for rehabilitation and hospice. Most seniors do not have long-term care insurance.

My mother's descent into poverty was both a shock and her salvation, unlocking access to government programs, but leaving gaps in care that, unfilled, ultimately resulted in her placement in skilled nursing.

My mother was educated and a small business owner. However, several of the life circumstances that resulted in her end-of-life situation befall many women. Women are uniquely at risk for ending their life in poverty due to factors like periods of absence from the labor market to care for children and family members, unequal pay, less opportunities for advancement, and victimization by fraudsters and even family members. Women also suffer from long term chronic illnesses including dementia at higher rates than men. Women also live longer than men and for some women, like my mother, living a long life with a chronic condition can result in impoverishment. In addition, the decline of defined benefit plan pensions in favor of self-managed retirement plans leave all seniors exposed to the vagaries of the market

In the next chapter we will explore a range of solutions to address the challenges which seniors, their families and caregivers encounter as the needs of aging outpace resources. We will explore the key dimensions to be considered—housing, healthcare and autonomy and make recommendations for maximizing the senior's experience in each of these areas. The chapter concludes with a timeline for decision making and planning. In chronicling Mary's journey and my own learning curve, I hope to leave you with a bread crumb trail to follow. There is no one size fits all approach, but there are key considerations and there are solutions.

CHAPTER FIVE

SOLUTIONS

My mother lived in the trailer from March 2016 to November 2017, when she entered skilled nursing. The mobile home park and the Placerville community had resources for seniors living alone, and I sought these out and signed my mother up with mixed success. As I initially reflected back on my mother's time in the trailer, I still had the "guilts"—the familiar feeling for caregivers that they could have done more to care for their parent and could have averted the falls or decline in health.

What I came to understand, though, is that the little trailer actually had many of the attributes that contribute to successful senior living: community, safety, and realistic autonomy. In navigating the trade-off between fostering independence and insuring safety, the trailer allowed my mother a high degree of independence with a safety net of support.

In unpacking my feelings about the solution, I also realized that part of my guilt came from my inability to meet my mother's middle-class expectations. She wasn't able to continue to live in the high-end independent living apartment that she'd loved and been promised by America's significant marketing machine, one that touts such options as the optimal lifestyle for seniors. For middle- and upper middle-class Americans, there are still a lot of class-based prejudices around living in a trailer park. Like any prejudice, it can serve to blind us to the innate value of the thing we dismiss.

The little trailer offered my mother a safe, clean place to live on her terms while surrounded by her familiar possessions and furniture. The trailer park also offered a lot of community support to help my mother stay independent. Though I had couched the trailer as a defeat in my mind, it was actually a win and creative solution to an incredibly complex problem that so many of us face.

The lay minister from the Catholic Church visited weekly to pray with my mother and offer the sacrament of Communion. This visit was a treasured part of my mother's week. A local evangelical Christian Church had adopted the mobile home park as a site where they provided ministry and practical services, such as gardening and painting. My mother welcomed the church members and appreciated their service.

So, my mother was housebound but certainly not alone. Her caregivers came four times per day—morning, lunch, dinner, and bedtime. One huge benefit of the mobile home park was that my mother's beloved caregiver from the independent living facility was able to continue to care for my mother. In addition, her aunt lived in the park and could also provide my mother with care. This was an ideal situation. Agencies frequently preclude short visits during the day requiring payment for an entire hour or more. I consider myself very lucky to have found independent caregivers willing to make short visits. It was doubly fortunate to have one of the caregivers as a neighbor.

The trailer pad was shaded by giant oaks. It bordered a creek and had a tidy little garden and a large, shaded deck. My mother enjoyed watching the birds at the birdfeeder and the deer and wild turkeys when they ventured into the park.

The neighbors in the mobile home park were another important source of socialization for my mother. They would drop in for a chat or even wave as they walked by. The mobile home park had an activity center and a lending library. My mother did not participate in the activities and potlucks but made good use of the library. There were many long-term residents of the trailer park. They had a well-established resident's association that organized the events at the activity center, coordinated work requests to park management, and advocated for park services with county Social Service agencies. With a high proportion of low-income residents, the county sent representatives to the park each year to sign residents up for the HEAP (Home Energy Assistance Program). In addition, my mother's neighbor organized weekly trips to local foodbanks to secure groceries to be shared amongst the residents. The food pantry was an important support to many residents.

Living independently with support in a close community was a very good solution for my mother. It afforded her a nice balance of autonomy and safety, one that can be hard to find in an institutional setting. Looking back on the history of the creation of assisted living facilities, the living situation I created for my mother was an embodiment of the vision held by Keren Wilson of Oregon, who worked to create the first assisted living facility in the United States here in Portland. It is instructive to look back at the original vision for assisted living and note how far we have moved from Wilson's vision to today's luxury units, which are vehicles for large investors but are not accessible for the majority of seniors.

KEREN WILSON'S VISION FOR SENIOR LIVING

Dr. Keren Wilson's quest to create a positive living situation for her own mother was the genesis of the concept of assisted living.

Ms. Wilson's mother entered a nursing home in 1969. Over the next ten years, as Wilson earned her PhD and worked for a trade association, she began to formulate a vision for senior housing not only for her own mother, but for all seniors, especially those with low income who were unable to pay for the services needed to keep them out of the limited options that were available for seniors at the time—institutional nursing homes and board and care homes which could be little more than "three hots and a cot."

Dr. Wilson once wrote: "Although both the design of the setting and the availability of supportive services would be important, personal control for residents also was crucial for individuals such as my mother. Thus, the model of assisted living I began working on in the early 1980s included a fully accessible apartment building with private living space, a full array of services, an emphasis on consumer autonomy, and the right to make choices regarding daily activities and health care."[66] For Wilson, there needed not be a tradeoff between providing health services to support daily living and privacy and autonomy.

Dr. Wilson described her vision for assisted living as having these attributes:

1. Housing. "A residential-style physical environment, pertaining to (a) a resident's private space and (b) public community spaces shared by all residents;

2. Health Services. A service capacity for (a) delivering routine services—both those amenable to being scheduled and those that could not be scheduled and (b) specialized health-related services; and

3. Autonomy. An operating philosophy emphasizing resident choice and normal lifestyles related to (a) the

governance of the resident's time, space, possessions, and contacts in his or her private space; and (b) decisions about accepting or rejecting medical care and other health-related care and services."[67]

In this chapter, we will use Wilson's framework for assisted living to describe the optimal living situation for seniors and to propose solutions to enable it. We will focus on the three areas—housing, autonomy, and health services. Knowing that most commercially available assisted living facilities are financially out of reach for most, this chapter provides solutions to support middle- and working-class seniors to creatively enable living arrangements that meet Dr. Wilson's vision. I recognize that personal and family-based solutions require creativity and still may be piecemeal in nature. What is truly needed is a comprehensive government solution for dependent elder care that moves beyond institutionalization and Medicaid to support seniors to live and age at home in their communities.

KEY AREA ONE: HOUSING

In his book *Being Mortal*, Atul Gawande describes a facility in Boston that epitomizes the type of facility envisioned by Dr. Wilson: NewBridge on the Charles River. "Instead of housing sixty people to a floor in shared rooms along an endless hospital corridor, New Bridge was divided into smaller pods housing no more than sixteen people," Gawande wrote. "Each pod was called a household and meant to function like one. The rooms were all private and were built around a common living area with a dining room, kitchen and activity room—like a home. Pets were welcomed in New Bridge and the facility shared its grounds with a private elementary school. The residents of New Bridge, who were able, worked in the school as tutors and librarians. New Bridge is not a facility for the wealthy—70 percent of New Bridge's residents had depleted their savings and relied on government assistance in order to pay for their stay." In addition, New Bridge benefited from significant philanthropic support from the Jewish community.

This example of an assisted living facility exemplifies the attributes that Keren Wilson identified as being key to enabling seniors to live as independently as possible, affording them agency and privacy but also the needed supports for the tasks of daily living.

First, this facility provided seniors with a private room. In Abraham Maslow's hierarchy of needs, safety and security, which includes the element of control that comes with having the ability to choose who comes into your space, is right above the basics for survival. Once you have food, water, and shelter, privacy is a basic need. In NewBridge, each resident had a private room. At the little trailer, my mother was afforded the ability to lock the door and to choose who came into her space. She had privacy and the security and familiarity of having her personal possessions, furniture, and collectables. While I would have wished that she allowed the Meals on Wheels volunteers to make their regular visits, she exercised her right to say no.

In addition to having a private space, Keren Wilson also envisioned that the ideal living space for seniors would include areas common for all residents to promote socializing. NewBridge had common areas including a kitchen and dining room, much like a home. The trailer park where my mother's trailer was located had a communal room which was used for bingo and regularly scheduled potlucks and a video and book lending library where the food bank was also located. My mother did not attend the bingo games or the potlucks but made regular use of the library.

Socialization and belonging are the next level of need on Maslow's hierarchy once food, shelter and safety needs have been addressed. Certainly, as families tour assisted living facilities, the alure of the activity center and dining room carry a lot of appeal.

The need for socialization can be met in many different ways, and the level of socialization is different for different people. Now that we have lived a year or more with the social isolation imposed on us by the COVID-19 pandemic, some of us find that we are doing fine in our apartments engaging over Zoom, while others are chafing to get out and reengage with the world. While I may have wanted my mother to be more social by attending Senior Day Care and accepting Meals on Wheels, for the most part I think she was content to spend more time alone with visits from neighbors and caregivers. Like arranging playdates for my children, my idea of friends for my mother may not have been her idea. However, as seniors and families are making choices about living arrangements, the ability to socialize is a key need for all of us that has to be addressed.

As you search for the right answer for your own family, consider these more specific attributes for senior housing identified by Dr. Wilson as well:

1. Architectural style commonly associated with places people have lived and that is thematically recognizable as residential (e.g., with building materials, design, and furnishings found in private homes).

2. Interior community space to accommodate recognized public functions (e.g., dining, socializing, shopping, receiving services).

3. Accommodation of cultural preferences for privacy (e.g., control over entry to and use of one's personal living

space, provisions for bathing and toilet use and for storing and preparing food in one's personal space, no requirements to share personal living space with others unless by choice).

4. Amenities in public and in personal space consistent with encouraging choice and continuity of life experiences (e.g., amount and type of community space, size of personal living space, temperature in personal living space).

5. Scale (size) and setting (location) congruent with older adults' life experiences in their own communities (e.g., rural, small town, suburban, or urban communities; different cultural communities).

6. Features to accommodate the individual's changing abilities (e.g., universal design features such as adjustable closets, lever door hardware; 100% wheelchair-accessible units and common space; roll-in showers to facilitate the ability to remain in the setting if the tenant chooses).[68]

LOCATION

Location is an important consideration for senior housing. It is foundational to the myriad of other decisions which must be made. Considerations for choosing a location is a function of family, money and lifestyle. Living in the family home or moving in with family or in an adjoining ADU (granny cottage) is one choice. For many, this choice is the least disruptive and potentially the lowest cost for the senior. Many factors could preclude this option. In my mother's case, her home was too large and too remote. Neither my brother nor I could take my mother into our homes or have the space to accommodate an ADU. Family dynamics may support multi-generational housing or preclude it.

Financial considerations impact the location decision as well. Moving my mother to Placerville was largely a financial consideration. The cost of the Independent Living facility in this rural area was half of what a similar facility cost in the expensive San Francisco Bay Area. It was initially a difficult move. At ninety years old, moving even three hours away was very disruptive. College educated and a business owner, my mother struggled to find common areas of interest with fellow residents who did not have the opportunities for travel and were interested in talking to her about gardening and baking.

Some seniors look to move even further away, to a resort-like environment in Arizona or Florida, or even further afield to Costa Rica or Mexico. The fastest growing city in the United States from the 2010 census to 2020 census was the Villages, a retirement community in Florida. The Villages' population grew by 39 percent over the decade.[69] Moving across the county to live in a retirement community is clearly a popular option. As seniors contemplate this kind of a move, considerations must include provisions for long-term care. The warm weather and amenities which make these locations desirable for younger seniors may be a problem when additional care is needed to accommodate growing heath care needs. Warm weather may be a welcome respite from cold winters, but climate change may pose its own challenges for warm weather locales. With mom or dad in Arizona, families may not be able to quickly get on a plane should an emergency arise.

The location decision is fundamental, both in the micro and macro sense. Macro decisions, moving to Florida or Costa Rica is clearly a fundamental decision that will have long ranging impacts not only on the senior but on entire families. In the micro sense, decisions about living with family or living independently in a senior's home community are equally impactful. Decisions made in a parent's early seventies may need to be re-visited and re-visited again as needs change. While senior housing mega-companies may tout the amenities that come with the resort like features of senior facilities, seniors may find that multi-generational living arrangements in the community may better meet their needs.

SOLUTION—ACCESSORY DWELLING UNITS (ADU'S)

Backyard ADU' are commonly referred to as "granny flats" since they are a good solution, allowing families to keep grandparents close but also allowing the privacy and autonomy that all family members appreciate. According to a recent Washington Post article, "Multigenerational living arrangements might improve financial resources, buffer stress, reduce loneliness, enhance intellectual sharing, and generate structural social capital, thereby elevating the level of one's health."[70]

Public policy changes from building code changes to enable ADUs, programs allowing for paid leave for elder care givers, and expanded training and higher caregiver wages would go a long way to make this healthy option more viable for seniors and their families. According to the Washington post, "The White House's American Jobs Plan calls for spending about $400 billion over eight years on "home- or community-based care" for the elderly." Other reports have stated that under the legislation, if approved, could pay up to 90 percent of the costs to states that receive and use grants to create plans for expanding their home-based services and boosting worker pay.[71]

Across the county, communities are challenging outdated zoning regulations to allow for multi-generational living with backyard ADUs and multi-plex housing. These zoning changes will not only make housing more affordable for young families but will allow seniors to downsize in order to stay in their home communities when the family home has grown too big or too expensive to manage.

One of the biggest barriers to the creation of these housing options is the minimum parking requirements that zoning regulations generally impose on new construction. These requirements drive up construction costs and spread out housing behind large swaths of parking lots. Across the country, cities are overturning these requirements to increase infill. Partnered with increased investments in public transportation, the zoning changes that will result in more affordable housing and accessible transportation will not only benefit first time buyers; they will create environments more conducive to seniors aging in place. Smaller dwelling units connected to shopping and medical services support seniors to stay in their home communities, too.

SOLUTION—COOPERATIVE HOUSING

Senior women are banding together creating alternative solutions for aging in place with the right mix of privacy and opportunities for community. According to ABC News, in Australia, where the public is facing a soaring rental market several women are turning to the newly formed foundation, Sharing With Friends: "The organisation, which is currently applying for charitable status, aims to provide an opportunity for women to buy into an affordable, custom-built home. The idea is that five women each invest $120,000, which pays for the construction of affordable purpose-built accommodation consisting of five private living quarters, with a communal laundry, library, and garden."[72]

Cooperative Housing for Seniors is also on the rise here in the United States, specifically in midwestern states like Minnesota, Iowa and Colorado. Senior Housing News reports that the number of senior co-ops has grew from 103 in 2013 to 125 in 2019, totaling 7,700 units with more than 10,500 residents.[73] Buying into a cooperative is a cost-effective way to enter senior housing, and can be an alternative to independent living and active adult communities. Residents purchase shares in a corporation that owns the building. These shares entitle stakeholders to lease a specific unit within a building and utilize common areas. Additionally, there is a monthly charge for assessments, maintenance, and repairs. Co-op living also gives residents a stake in how a community is managed, similar to a traditional homeowners' association.

In Pennsylvania, Thistledown Cooperative Living House offers a month-to-month lease with a sliding scale rent, based on a percentage of residents' income. Each member of the household has their own bedroom and bathroom and share common living spaces. The house combats isolation by creating a household that connects and functions as a family, sharing tasks and responsibilities and offering an informal support network.[74]

According to Senior Housing News, for decades, retirees buying mobile homes banded together to create ownership cooperatives before private investors and REITs made the product a tradable, institutional-grade investment class. Sadly, we are fast losing one of the most practical, available, and affordable options for senior housing as investment conglomerates by up senior mobile home parks. The option to simply re-locate to another park is not really viable, as the cost to move a manufactured home can be as much as $20,000 and park spaces are at a premium. Knowing this, absentee landlords can turn a deaf ear even to the most well-organized group of tenants.

When my mother moved into the mobile home park, it was a family-owned business with an active homeowner's association. While the rent had increased, it was still very affordable, and many tenants had owned their homes in the park for years. When I purchased my mother's trailer, the space rent was less than $500 per month. Long-term tenants paid even less. While there was ongoing dialogue about maintenance issues, the active tenant's association put enough pressure on the family to ensure that the park remained a safe and well-maintained environment for the one hundred or so resident families.

Like so many other senior parks across America, the owners decided to retire, and their children had no interest in running the park. Other senior parks in the area had already been sold to institutional investors, and the residents saw steady increases in their rent. My mother had already moved into the skilled nursing facility, but I remained close with many of her neighbors. Michelle E. Smith, my mother's closest neighbor, even decided to run for the presidency of the local manufactured homeowner's association to ensure that the park tenants were well represented in Sacramento as they lobbied for laws to make it easier for park residents to purchase their parks and to pump the brakes on the commodification of what is a practical, popular, and affordable housing option for seniors. The seniors in the mobile home park where my mother lived, made an attempt to secure funding to purchase the park. At the time of this writing, their offer had not been accepted but the park had not yet been sold to another buyer.

For seniors, housing is a key decision. So many senior living options leave seniors vulnerable to inflation as rents escalate to ensure investor profits. Other options, especially skilled nursing facilities, may lack the privacy, autonomy, or socialization that is key to meeting their needs. When evaluating senior housing options, look past the gloss and distraction of independent living apartments and look to find the resources in your home communities which offer a cooperative ownership model where seniors, not investors, make decisions and re-invest profits back into the facility. Cooperative housing can also offer the opportunity to get involved in governance or other opportunities to volunteer to help fellow residents or in the community. Multi-generational housing options including ADUs are also a good solution for families who have the space to keep seniors close but enjoy the privacy which comes from having separate spaces. Many municipalities are revising their building codes to allow these in-fill units.

These options, which may be the healthiest and most cost effective for seniors, are under constant threat from profit seeking investors. Mobile home parks and senior co-op housing are all targets for today's investor class just as Assisted Living facilities were commodified in the 1990s. As seniors look for optimal housing options for themselves and their loved ones, know that increasing the availability of innovative housing solutions will require tough policy battles at the local, state and national levels. In addition to sourcing the solution for your family, seniors and their advocates need to engage with lawmakers to make these options more available for all.

KEY AREA TWO: AUTONOMY

In the set of key attributes for assisted living as characterized by Dr. Wilson, the focus is on human dignity or the "values orientation to preserve resident's self-worth."[75] Dr. Wilson describes an optimal environment as having the following attributes:

a. A focus on ability as opposed to disability (e.g., to support the highest level of independence possible to meeting self-needs and to assist in motivating individuals to set personal goals for increased ability for self-care).

b. Focus on decision making, both decisional and executional autonomy (e.g., to offer choices in a way that encourages, facilitates, and respects decisions at all levels of importance)

c. Focus on personalization (e.g., to recognize the uniqueness of each individual and to capture that individuality in a negotiated service agreement in partnership with the consumer and his or her family).

d. Focus on reciprocity (e.g., to recognize and promote mutual respect, dignity, and responsibility to be shared by the consumer, the caregiver, and those of special importance to the consumer, such as the family).

e. Focus on boundaries (e.g., to uphold the personal boundaries related to privacy involving emotional intimacy, information, and the physical body; to use techniques like managed risk agreements as a means to identify and establish boundaries around decision and subsequent behaviors that might cause harm to the person).[76]

Dr. Wilson saw the optimal environment for seniors as one that provides the highest level of personal autonomy in decision making, self-care and privacy. In her final statement, Dr. Wilson acknowledges the reality of risk and the need to "establish boundaries around decisions that may cause harm." This acknowledgement, for me, defined one of the central issues faced by my role as a caregiver—how to balance the recognition of my mother's need as an adult to make her own decisions and to structure her life in a way that was meaningful to her, balanced with the need for risk management. How best should I help her to manage the very real risks that came with aging and her disability progression? How should I support her lifestyle preferences even when I could foresee that there may be risk involved—either immediate or in the long term?

As a caregiver, the urge to tip the balance toward risk aversion was very strong. I sometimes wished I could cocoon my mother in bubble wrap to prevent the next fall. I certainly wished that we could afford a 24-hour caregiver to enable her to live at home for a longer period of time. Wishful ideation could sometimes give way to protracted disagreements. When does support for one's favorite charities give way to concerns over financial abuse? How should I support my mother's autonomous decision making at the grocery store when the cart is filling with processed food, cookies and ice cream and she is an insulin dependent diabetic?

SOLUTION—LEGAL FOUNDATIONS

These decisions were the speed bumps on the road to the bigger and more fundamental decisions that families and caregivers make on behalf of their loved ones—questions of life or death as documented in a Healthcare Power of Attorney and decisions over one's financial assets as documented in a Will and/or Trust and in a Financial Power of Attorney (FPOA). These legal documents are how our legal, financial, and healthcare systems all work to give caregivers the right to make decisions on behalf of their loved ones. They must be in place to allow even a spouse to access medical records, pay bills, and obtain key documents in the event that a senior is incapacitated and unable to do this for themselves.

Having a Healthcare Power of Attorney document allowed me to speak with my mother's doctor to clarify instructions, to talk to the nurse when my mother was admitted to the Emergency Room, and to engage with hospital discharge planners. Without this document, HIPAA rules designed to protect patient privacy would have prevented me from having these important conversations. In addition to the Healthcare Power of Attorney document, the state of California has a form called an Advanced Directive. This document provides guidance to emergency responders and healthcare providers in the event that the patient is incapacitated. The Advanced Directive was posted on my mother's refrigerator and was on file at the local hospital. It gave explicit instructions as to her wishes with regard to the extent to which she wished to have medical intervention in the event of an emergency.

I strongly advise caregivers and families to get the senior in their care to prepare and execute a Healthcare Power of Attorney and an Advance Directive. It will be very difficult, if not impossible, to provide care and interact with hospital and medical professionals without these. Fortunately, my mother saw the benefit of having me in the loop with her doctor and when she was in the hospital and readily agreed to sign the necessary documents to enable my participation. It was not the case with financial decision making.

An entire industry is in place to provide advice to seniors on estate planning. I am not a lawyer and recommend that if families or dependent seniors have real property or significant financial assets that they engage an attorney to establish the necessary legal documents to enable financial decision making to take place should a senior become incapacitated. My mother did have a trust in place but named herself as the Trustee. I never did have the legal power to transact financial business on behalf of my mother. I was also the Executor of her will, however she died intestate, meaning that there was no money to be disbursed to creditors or those named in her will upon her death.

Short of having the legal power to transact business on my mother's behalf, we were able to work out a system that allowed me to help her to manage her budget and pay her bills. Admittedly, this was only the case when she had virtually run out of money and was living on her Social Security benefits alone. Had we implemented this plan earlier, it may have stretched her assets for a longer period of time. I used a time when my mother had a short hospitalization to pick up her mail, sort the bills and bring the bills and the checkbook to the hospital for her to sign before sending. She was comfortable with this process since she was still in control. In the next step, I took her checkbook home with me, and we wrote checks only when we were together. Note that I did not have any special legal authority, and she had agreed to this process. This could be a good middle ground for seniors and their families who are struggling with handing over financial decision rights.

While my mother passed in 2018, and the internet revolution was well underway, she was very old school. She paid all her bills via check and dropped them in the "snail" mailbox. Online bill pay was not an option for her. Technology can be a great support for caregivers. With authorization, banks will allow authorized parties to conduct financial transactions on the part of the account holder. This authorization can be blanket or limited to certain types of transactions. Most banks have their own forms for this. It is a limited version of a Financial Power of Attorney (FPOA). You do not have to have a blanket FPOA in place. If a dependent senior is resistant to relinquishing all financial control, a bank or account specific FPOA can be a good first step. Combined with online bill pay, this is a good way to help a senior manage their finances while retaining autonomy.

SOLUTION—TECHNOLOGY

Today's seniors are much more technology savvy and more interested in using technology to enable them to live safely at home, albeit with some significant reservations and limitations. According to a recent AARP survey, seniors see technology as being a key enabler in three key areas—security, heath care and wellness, and maintaining social connections.[77] Investors are also showing increased interest in "agetech."

"According to Crunchbase, the amount of annual venture funding for eldercare has grown 10x since 2011 and surpassed $1 billion in 2020."[78] Here are a few ways in which technology can be part of the answer to enable seniors to live independently at home or in their community.

For years, I went every week to help my mother grocery shop—first in San Mateo when she was in independent living and then making the three-hour drive to Placerville. At the time, living in a rural area, on-line shopping and grocery delivery were not available. What a help it would have been to maintain an on-line grocery list, click a few boxes, enable payment, and have groceries delivered weekly or on an as-needed basis. Note that not all grocery delivery services accept EBT or government benefits, and chains that do accept these benefits may not in all locations.

While some may debate the merits of on-line shopping and the demise of main street retailers, there is no doubt that it would have been very helpful to be able to buy medical devices, medical supplies, cleaning products, and home goods online for my mother and to have them delivered! To do this, a caregiver has to have the authorization to make credit card purchases on behalf of the dependent senior. Even if we could have done this together to ensure proper authorization, on-line shopping and delivery would have been a great assist for my mother.

Home security, including fall detection, is another key area in which technology can assist seniors to live safely at home. According to the AARP tech study, "Older individuals are particularly interested in using smart home and security tech to see who is at the front door (59%), automatically shut off appliances (42%), control a thermostat (38%), detect a fall or get emergency help (39%), and monitor doors and windows (48%)."[79]

For a senior, having the heat or air conditioner automatically turn on and off and adjust means less getting up and down, reducing fall risk, especially in the early morning or at night. An open window is not only a security risk; a cold breeze can interrupt a night's rest. Programmable thermostats, appliances, and home security devices can mean that grandma can wake up in a warm house with a warm pot of coffee already brewed. Visitors can be screened without getting up to answer the door.

Fall-detection devices have been on the market for years. The refrain of "help, I've fallen, and I can't get up" is sure to be a familiar one. I purchased a wearable button and a call service for my mother when she lived in the trailer. There are many services on the market that operate in a similar fashion. If a senior falls, they press a button that activates the device to call a help desk. The worker queries if the senior needs assistance and either calls 911 or the designated caregiver. However, cost can be a barrier. According to a recent Forbes Health article "medical alert systems can cost more than $100 and require monthly subscription fees from $20 to $55, plus more for additional services like automatic fall detection. Medicare doesn't cover medical alert systems."[80] Some

Medicare Advantage programs may cover fall detection devices, but coverage varies.

While today's generation of parents are growing more comfortable with the use of cameras in nursery and daycare settings, older adults may balk at the notion of being watched. However, some adult children living away from their aging parents have found comfort in being able to see mom or dad in the living room or kitchen, knowing that they are safe and well. There are several products on the market for remote monitoring of older adults. Here are two examples:

1. **Aeyesafe Monitoring Alert System** is a sound and thermal monitoring system that provides current and historical data. It doesn't require human intervention for monitoring, which encourages independence. The system allows the user to request help if needed through voice activation, and it uses artificial intelligence sensors, which provide human-like monitoring.

   In using heat and sound monitors, the device provides:

   - Body temperature analysis
   - Sleep analysis
   - Danger detection
   - Abnormal behavior detection.

   Aeyesafe isn't a wearable device—it's voice-activated and operates from a distance with a substantial battery and power supply, and it reports emergencies or abnormalities directly to the caregiver.

2. **Alarm.com Wellness** is a partner to **Alarm.com**, a home security system. The two systems work together

to provide comprehensive insight into the behavior and safety of seniors living on their own. The tracker can alert caregivers of abnormal behavior patterns—such as leaving the home at odd hours or wandering—in addition to monitoring light, temperature, and security settings. The system may be paired with personal emergency response (PERS) pendants.

The tracker provides info on:

- Activity levels
- Bathroom use
- Eating habits
- Medication management
- Sleep patterns
- Fires, intruders, or medical emergencies.[81]

In addition, the ubiquitous iPhone and Smart Watch can monitor blood oxygen levels, sleep patterns, heart rhythms, and steps walked.

Falls, burns, and medication errors are all too common occurrences that can put a senior in the hospital. While changes to the home environment like removing tripping hazards and reducing clutter are the primary way to reduce falls, remote sensor options are useful to quickly detect a fall and summon help.

I was very fearful of the potential for burns and fire posed by the gas stove in my mother's trailer. In her independent living apartment, she had left the electric stove on more than once burning pots and pans but mercifully not herself. Gas posed a much higher level of risk. In the trailer, I removed the gas stove and replaced it with a microwave, toaster oven, and electric kettle for her use. The caregiver could also operate the hot plate. There are products on the market today which could have made the kitchen a safer place.

There are products on the market today to reduce the opportunity for burns by automatically shutting off appliances. HomeCare Magazine profiled a few such the kitchen safety devices, including stovetop sensors that automatically turn off an electric stove to prevent food from catching fire and potentially causing a house fire. Their favorite brands, FireAvert and CookStop, monitor for motion and unattended pots or are triggered by smoke. Another product, Safe T Sensor, is engineered to help prevent microwave fires by interrupting power to the microwave at the first sign of smoke. SmartRange was their ideal safety solution for all glass-top electric ranges with its ability to monitor changes in the range's cooking temperature, signal pre-fire alarms, and automatically shut the range off if needed.[82]

Skipped medication or errors in administering medication are also a common problem which can result in hospitalization. There are a range of products on the market which can assist seniors in medication management. Subscription services sort medications into daily dose packaging and deliver them to the patient's door. The most familiar of these is PillPak, acquired by Amazon in June of 2018. This Amazon service accepts all forms of insurance. There is no cost for the service and customers don't pay for shipping. It seems almost too good to be true. I can remember sorting my mother's medications and refilling each of the small container bins during visits. It was confusing for me, and impossible for my mother. Since this service is dependent on insurance billing and communication with prescribing doctors, the biggest set of consumer complaints with PillPak are late shipments or billing errors due to the complexities of our healthcare system.

Once medications have been sorted and delivered, the last mile is to get the senior to take them. Here also, technology has come up with some solutions. AARP recently profiled two technology solutions to remind seniors to take their medication.[83] Reminder Rosie is a voice-activated talking clock that tells you to take your medicine at a certain time. Of note, Reminder Rosie does not need to be connected to the internet to work. Another option is Med-Minder—a digital pill dispenser that looks like a regular seven-day model. The dispenser flashes when it's pill time, then beeps if the medicine isn't taken. Still no luck? A prerecorded voice from, say, a grandchild, reminds Grandma to take them. If she doesn't, she gets a call, and a family member receives an email, text or call.

Ride share services are another common technology that's a great enabler for seniors. When my mother entered the first independent living facility in San Mateo, she gave up her car within the year and never drove again. The facility had a bus which took the residents to special events and on a pre-set route to grocery stores and to the mall. For doctor's appointments there was a car and driver which could be scheduled in advance. I also took my mother to doctor's appointments. These days, ride share services can be a solution. Schedule a Lyft or Uber, and a senior can go where they want, when they want. All Lyft and Uber drivers pass a background check. In some major metro areas, Lyft and Uber also offer wheelchair accessible transportation and rides in which the driver is alerted that the passenger may need extra time to get in and out of the car. Note that a smartphone is required to use Lyft or Uber and availability of drivers may be limited in rural areas.

If a senior is struggling to use a smartphone, there is a technology solution, however. GoGoGrandparent is a phone-based go-between that charges a small fee to arrange Ubers and Lyfts for older riders. Relatives and caretakers can use GoGoGrandparent to call in a ride and monitor the progress

Using technology, we can get grandma home delivered groceries, medications, and transportation and support safety with security devices, fall alerts, and medication management. COVID-19 has also greatly expanded the use of telemedicine, so routine doctor visits can be conducted via the internet. I recently had an unexpected allergic reaction to shellfish. I was able to upload pictures of the hives and a brief description of my other symptoms, and in less than an hour a prescription was called in to my local pharmacy. Telemedicine is the wave of the future for the provision of health services. Bringing the doctor to the senior reduces the risk of contagion in a busy medical center and solves for the challenges with transportation to and from the doctor.

One more area where technology can be a great assist to seniors living alone are apps that promote human connection including gaming, video conferencing, and social media applications. According to an AARP survey 44 percent of adults over 50 years old played video games in 2019 at least once a month. The AARP survey includes players of all sorts of computer or video games, and the majority say they play puzzle and logic games, such as Sudoku or Words With Friends. But Alison Bryant, senior vice president of AARP Research, says a 2020 survey by MRI-Simmons found that about a quarter of gamers over 50 play multiplayer games using a video system and one-third of that group identifies as medium or heavy players."[84]

In 2018 Facebook, now Meta, launched the Facebook Portal, now the Meta Portal. The device simplifies the set up and functionality of video conferencing with an "always in frame" feature that tracks the presenter and focuses the camera to reduce background distractions. The portal supports most common video conferencing software and seniors can start a video call with a simple voice command instead of a complicated log-on process. The portal supports photo sharing, group movie watching, and story time, a feature that "brings children's stories to life with music, animation and AR effects," according to Meta. Seniors are a key customer segment for this technology from Facebook and are prominently featured on the webpage describing the product. Demonstrating the volatility of the senior tech market, Meta announced in June 2022 that they would no longer release new versions of the portal but would continue to support the 1.3 million users who had already purchased the product. However, Google has brought a similar product to market.

The Google and Meta portals support Amazon Alexa, virtual assistant software from Amazon that is enabled through a speaker and is fast becoming a coordinating hub for many of the technology assists mentioned above including controlling home security devices, calling ride-share companies, managing appliances, and setting medication reminders. Alexa can respond to simple queries about the weather or news, play music, set alarms and reminders, order groceries, and can even play games. Alexa can also serve as a phone and can act as a control for smart home appliances: "Alexa, turn on the coffee maker." Alexa can be personalized to repeat familiar personal stories, for example "Alexa, tell me about how we met."

In December 2021, Amazon launched Alexa Together, which is, according to the company, "designed to offer a minimally invasive way to use Amazon's voice assistant and associated Echo speakers to both assist and keep tabs on an elderly loved one or other person who requires a caregiver." Alexa Together is a subscription service that costs $199 per year that uses sensors for monitoring, the value proposition being that sensor feeds are less invasive than camera or video-based monitoring. Alexa Together also has an emergency alert feature which enables voice activated commands to call an emergency helpline to summon first responders or a caregiver.

Alexa Together is specifically marketed to seniors and their families and is a clear indication that the technology giants are pursuing the "agetech" market to support seniors to age at home. Looking to the future, Amazon has said its convinced that everyone will have a robot of some sort in their home in the next five to ten years. Amazon's Astro is already on the market. The small robot functions like a robot vacuum, delivering mobile Echo capability. Imagine a small robot following you from room to room to respond to your every query. The vision of the future promised in our childhood TV shows like Star Trek and the Jetsons is coming to pass complete with home robots and self-driving cars. Of course, there was always the dystopian version of future technology like HAL from 2001: A Space Odyssey.

Technology solutions are not a utopia and may serve to widen economic and physical divisions in our society which could far outweigh the practical benefits. Privacy concerns loom large for the use of technology for seniors, and there are significant privacy concerns with voice enabled assistants like Alexa. By definition these devices are always on, even when they are not awake, the devices are constantly listening, although not always transmitting. There are many well publicized and scary instances of Alexa gone awry from sharing private conversations to random and inappropriate vocalizations from the device.

Installation of any type of monitoring system should only be done by mutual consent. The senior should be made aware of the system, how it works and how to turn it off. Video or audio monitoring should not take place in the bathroom or bedroom, places where privacy is expected, however a call button or other fall detection device may be important in these spaces. If there is a caregiver in the home, their consent should also be obtained prior to installation of a monitoring system. Ideally this consent should be in writing.

In addition to practical privacy concerns, there are data privacy concerns. What is happening to all of the conversations that have been recorded by voice assistants? Machine learning-based voice assistant software like Alexa continually stores audio in order to use it to better train its algorithms. Human employees intervene as well, helping fine-tune the digital assistants to listen and respond more accurately. Yes, humans are listening to recordings from home virtual assistants if only to help the assistants get smarter. One can imagine the dystopian uses of recorded conversations in the hands of hackers, predatory vendors, or government agencies. Consumers should also be aware of the extent to which the use of home recordings can be used to micro target advertising. It can already seem that you might have just mentioned a topic in a conversation and related ads start popping up on your social media or news feed. The decision to introduce a virtual home assistant should include research into the safeguards to protect consumer privacy.

The promise of technology as a societal leveler, elevating life for everyone has yet to come to pass. Another concern about the use of technology for seniors is that is simply not available for many. Broadband internet connection is still not ubiquitous across the country. In many rural areas, there are huge swaths of regions where there is no service. Incredibly, a neighbor in Placerville, could only access the internet by satellite when all of the rest of the houses on the block had the option of high-speed cable internet. The service provider stopped offering service two hundred feet from the house. No amount of pleading or lobbying could influence the service provider to extend the range of service. Significantly, a study conducted in conjunction with Cornell University found that "Nearly 22 million American seniors do not have wireline broadband access at home, representing 42 percent of the nation's over-65 population. A review of existing digital inclusion efforts targeting seniors found a hodgepodge of offerings, with large sections of the country served by no significant low-cost offerings or age-friendly initiatives."[85]

A study by Humana in partnership with OATS (Older Adults Technology Services) found that "older adults with less than a high school degree or an income of less than $25,000 are 10 times more likely than the general population to be offline. The report found, Black and Latino older adults are, respectively, more than 2.5 and 3.6 times more likely than the general population to lack computer access." In addition, older adults who are single (2.7 times as likely) or live in rural areas (1.6 times as likely) have elevated odds of lacking home internet service.[86] Medicaid enrollees were found to be 2.7 times as likely not to be likely online. Increasingly for seniors the benefits of technology assists are simply not available for the very populations that could benefit the most. For low- income seniors in rural areas, access to telehealth could be lifesaving.

Getting seniors on-line will not require a moonshot, but it will require government coordination and oversight of service providers. The current patchwork of subsidized programs targeting seniors leaves swaths of the population unserved. The infrastructure bill approved by Congress and signed into legislation by President Biden in 2021 includes funding for a number of programs that can help with online access and connectivity. The bill also allocates $2.7 billion for digital literacy training as the last mile for many seniors is training on using basic digital tools.

Enabling autonomy, self-care and privacy were, for Keren Wilson, key foundational elements for successful senior living. For caregivers, ensuring that the right foundational legal documents are in place to protect the senior in their care and to ensure the ability to communicate with healthcare, financial and legal professionals is baseline. At minimum the senior needs to complete an Advance Directive so that their wishes for end-of-life care can be respected. A Healthcare Power of Attorney is also important to allow caregivers and other loved ones to communicate with doctors and hospital personnel. HIPAA laws are very strict, and medical staff will not engage with family members unless they have written permission to do so. A Financial Power of Attorney document will allow a trusted caregiver to transact business on behalf of a senior. However, there are practical ways to work together with the senior in your care should they be reluctant to sign over legal authority over their finances.

Technology can be a significant enabler of autonomy and security for a senior. Home security, fall detection, automated shutoffs for appliances and timers to turn lights, heating, and air conditioning on and off can make independent living safer and more comfortable. Online shopping and delivery services can bring food and needed supplies directly to the home. Automated medication reminders can ensure that prescriptions are being administered. On-line bill pay can make sure that financial obligations are being met. Video chat, gaming, and voice assistants can be a source of socializing and entertainment for the homebound. Technology is not a panacea. The benefits cannot be overlooked when creating a plan for independent living, but the drawbacks should not be minimized. Availability, cost, and privacy concerns should be addressed not only by families but by a comprehensive legislation that could ensure that all seniors have access, and that data security and privacy concerns are addressed.

KEY AREA THREE: HEALTH SERVICES

The third key priority area for seniors is health services. Since I was able to help my mother solve for housing, the vast majority of her budget when living in the little trailer went for medical expenses not covered by Medicare and for caregivers. Health care expenses are the biggest budgeting unknown for seniors. The significant gaps in Medicare leave seniors vulnerable to not getting the care they need, to medical bankruptcy and ultimately to poverty. My mother's need for round the clock care could not be provided without reducing her to the poverty level required to access Medicaid.

Healthcare spend has outpaced economic growth in the U.S. The increase in the cost of healthcare, housing, and education are major factors leading to economic challenges for the working and middle class. According to the Peterson-KFF Health System Tracker: "On a per capita basis, health spending has increased over *31-fold* in the last four decades, from $353 per person in 1970 to $11,582 in 2019. In constant 2019 dollars, the increase was about 6-fold, from $1,848 In 1970 to $11,582 in 2019."[87]

Gaps in Medicare coverage leave seniors to pay out of pocket for dental care and hearing aids. In addition, even with Medicare Part D, the cost of prescription drugs leaves seniors vulnerable to uncovered expenses. Even with a medigap insurance plan, there is a period of time commonly referred to as the "donut hole" when a senior will have reached the coverage ceiling for Medicare plus Medicare supplement before catastrophic coverage kicks in. These costs alone can bankrupt a senior. However, the biggest expense for most, and certainly for my mother, is the cost for caregivers. Medicare does not cover the cost of long-term care or for caregivers.

Going back to Keren Wilson's original vision for assisted living, the provision of health services was the third of the three priority areas. Dr. Wilson describes the dimensions of a comprehensive health services for seniors as follows:

a. Ability to provide assistance with activities of daily living and instrumental activities of daily living when needed and wanted (e.g., capacity to meet scheduled and unscheduled needs at a time agreed to by the consumer by a universal worker trained to accommodate most needs).

b. Appropriate interventions to manage the effects of chronic disease or disability (e.g., the ability to provide health-related services associated with assessment of condition; plan negotiated with the consumer and/or the family for needed services, management of medication use, direct or delegated nursing treatments; follow-through with ordered therapies; and end-of-life palliative care).

c. Arrangement for treatment of acute care episodes and mental health issues (e.g., identification, coordination, and monitoring of condition to ensure timely intervention in the assisted living community or by transfer to another setting for specialized treatments; hospital, psychiatric unit, skilled nursing facility, rehabilitation center).

d. Attention to all aspects of well-being (e.g., emotional support of individual tenant and his or her family, opportunities to form new relationships and to engage in activities of personal interest, opportunities to be spiritual in a way acceptable to the individual, opportunities to experience continued personal growth).

e. Responsibility for the coordination (case management) of services needed for enhanced well-being (e.g., arrangement of services of any type not specifically available in the assisted living community, oversight of transitional events such as move in and move out).[88]

It is almost hard to envision that this healthcare utopia could be possible. We, as a society, have come to expect so much less from our healthcare system and from our government. As we discussed in chapter three, as a society we make this work by relying on the non-paid labor of female relatives, underpaid caregivers, or making do with less care for seniors than what is needed to be safe and healthy. Solving for the many gaps for the provisioning of health services goes beyond the resourcefulness of individual seniors and their families. Large scale systemic change is need. While we work to lobby our elected officials to enact change, families will have to have strategies to cover the gaps.

SOLUTION—FAMILY AGREEMENT

One solution for families is the creation of a family agreement. A family agreement is a formal document in which care expectations, arrangements for the provision of care, and payment expectations are clearly spelled out. It is a living document and will need to be updated as the care needs of a senior change. As we have learned and experienced, there is an expectation that daughters and other female relatives will take on the responsibility of caregiving without compensation and without a clear definition of the scope of work. By leaving the scope of work undefined and not setting an expectation for re-imbursement, caregivers are vulnerable to the financial exploitation and burnout we have explored in previous chapters.

Initiating the creation of a family agreement can engender push back in many families. It works for most that expectations for the provision of care remain amorphous and that caregiving is presumed to be a free service. It certainly works for the members of the family who are not contributing to care and in some instances, it may also work for the senior who does not want to acknowledge their level of dependency and their financial vulnerability. I know that in my case, I just did what was in front of me as my mother's care needs grew, and her bank account was depleting. I took the time off work that was necessary to ensure that she got to her doctor appointments and paid for her housing and any bills that Social Security, Medicare, and other government programs did not cover. So, this advice is definitely do as I say, not as I did.

A family agreement helps to identify gaps in a care plan. A daughter and paid caregivers may not be able to cover all care needs, leaving areas where care is simply not provided. For my mother, frequent falls became a red flag that she needed more than four visits from a caregiver each day. Round-the-clock care was needed, and we had to make a change. Fairness is another driver for the creation of a family care plan. While the provision of care between siblings and other relatives may never be equal, documenting the division of labor and resources in a care plan can go a long way to making it transparent. In addition to these very real benefits, a family care plan can address two important legal and financial issues for seniors, their families, and for caregivers.

It may come as a surprise, but more than half of U.S. states have filial responsibility laws. Filial responsibility means that children are legally responsible for providing for the necessities of life for their parent. These states are shown in the table below, from Harbor Life Settlements, which states: "Know that these laws can be very different from state to state. Georgia's statute, for example, simply states that a child who's able must support an impoverished parent. The Arkansas law requires an adult child to provide specifically for a parent's mental health needs, but only when that child has the means to pay and the services are not covered by insurance.

In Virginia, you and your siblings are financially responsible for medical bills including long-term care—but you are no longer responsible for that long-term care bill after your parent has been institutionalized for 60 months or more."

States with Filial Responsibility Laws		
Alaska	Louisiana	Oregon
Arkansas	Massachusetts	Pennsylvania
California	Mississippi	Rhode Island
Connecticut	Montana	South Dakota
Delaware	Nevada	Tennessee
Georgia	New Jersey	Utah
Indiana	North Carolina	Vermont
Iowa	North Dakota	Virginia
Kentucky	Ohio	West Virginia

Before we have a collective heart attack, know that these laws are rarely invoked since successful application for Medicaid ensures that care is provided for seniors who cannot take care of their own needs. There have been two landmark cases in which families have been held accountable for the skilled nursing care of a parent. According to Harbor Life Settlements, "The best-known filial law case is Health Care & Retirement Corporation of America v. Pittas of 2012. At issue was a $93,000 nursing home bill that an elderly patient did not pay. Upon her release from the home, the woman left the country. The nursing home then sued her son who was still in the U.S. The courts ruled that the son was financially able and therefore responsible for paying the bill."

In this case, the son was held liable since the senior was no longer in the U.S. and not able to qualify for Medicaid. In another case a North Dakota Supreme Court found Elden Linderkamp liable for his parents' unpaid medical debt—a balance of $104,000 owed to a nursing home. In this case, the parents had previously sold property to Elden and his wife for less than market value; the nursing home claimed that the transaction was intended to keep the property out of creditors' hands. The court found Linderkamp and his wife liable for the debt.[89]

These cases, while rare, illustrate an important legal consideration for the creation of a family agreement. A family agreement provides a documentation trail for reimbursement of care-related expenses in the event that a senior needs to qualify for Medicaid. Without documentation, money paid to a family member for payment of wages to provide for the care of a senior, or any other transfer of assets between a senior and a family member could jeopardize the ability for the senior to qualify for Medicaid without incurring a waiting period. The "look back" period for most states is five years. To qualify for Medicaid which includes both skilled nursing and IHSS services, the state will examine the financial records of the applying senior looking for evidence of a transfer of assets during the previous five years. Should there be proof that the family is looking to hide asset transfers, the state will calculate the amount of money which should be available for care, divide it by the average cost of care in the state and determine the time period for which the senior will need to wait in order to be eligible for Medicaid. Imagine that your mother needs skilled nursing care and, due to an undocumented asset transfer, she is subject to a six-month waiting period! Yet, it is understandable that such a rule exists. Without it, seniors needing care could transfer all of their assets to their heirs and leave the state with the bill for their care.

According to the American Bar Association, a comprehensive family agreement should include the following:

1. **Include a start date for services.** The agreement should include a specific start date for when service begins. This date should not be retroactive. Generally, agreements can be for a specific period of time or indefinitely. If the arrangement is long-term, consider reviewing the agreement, services, and compensation on an annual basis.

2. **Detail the services included in the agreement.** Agreements can be very detailed as to providing non-medical care only, such as cooking meals, doing housekeeping and laundry, or providing transportation to appointments. Activities of daily living include more personal assistance such as bathing, toileting, transferring, walking, exercising, medication reminders, feeding, dressing changes, etc. Understand the scope of the services needed and determine the caretaker's comfort level and skill level. Is the caregiver up to the task of performing these tasks?

   Consult with a physician-obtain a medical opinion of whether their needs can realistically be met in a home setting. The physician may assist with determining how much care is necessary and assist in a mental capacity assessment.

   An alternative method of creating a care plan is to hire a licensed geriatric care manager to visit the adult at home and conduct an assessment of their health and needs. There is a fee associated with an assessment which varies by state and region. The geriatric care manager may also be retained on a monthly or as-needed basis to provide an in-home assessment between physician office visits.

3. **Make a legal plan.** If there is no estate plan in place, now is the time to address the need for Powers of Attorney, possible guardianship, wills, trusts, and health care directives. The mental capacity of a loved one will dictate what documents may be executed.

4. **Make a financial plan.** What are the assets and resources in the estate? Caregiving agreements are often tied to Supplemental Security Income (SSI) or Medicaid planning. There may be a spend-down scenario where using assets to legitimately pay for a family caregiver enables a loved one to not jeopardize SSI or Medicaid eligibility.

    Identify assisted living or skilled facilities to consider for Plan B when providing care at home is no longer an option. Consult the admissions director about the levels of care provided, private-pay requirements, and acceptance of SSI/Medicaid payments when assets have been exhausted. Many communities require a period of private pay prior to accepting Medicaid. Families that wait until there is no money left limit their choices and accessibility.

5. **Agree on compensation.** Conduct a salary survey of home services agencies in the area to assist in the determination of compensation for the caregiver. Agencies charge a higher rate because they absorb all the responsibility of an employer: payroll taxes, unemployment, workers' compensation, supervision, training, licensing requirements, and more. Private-hire caregivers do not carry the same financial responsibility and are less expensive but come at a greater risk of liability.

Review the proposed compensation with the loved one and other family members as some may be sensitive to how this arrangement might affect the overall family dynamics.

6. **Consider caretaker leave needs.** Respite, vacation, and illness coverage are important in any employment scenario—consider paid vacation or paid time off (PTO) for caretaker illnesses. What is the back-up care plan for the loved one? Another family member may step in or the caretaker may need to contract with a local agency for back-up support. Agencies generally need 24-48 hours to initiate a service agreement and to provide a qualified caregiver.

7. **Keep a daily log or note archive.** Daily notes or journaling provide the supporting documentation to justify the care provided; include the care provided and any payments received. These notes are valuable to communicate to other family members about the care provided and to assist in an application for Medicaid. Ensure that you have a consistent, reliable way to store these notes. Consider storing all important documents in a binder and add supplemental information along the way.

8. **Review and update the care plan.** It is recommended that the caretaker and the loved one review the plan at least once a year. If a loved one has a medical event and requires hospitalization, it may be helpful to review the care plan for any changes in care needs especially with medication and any post-hospitalization therapy requirements.

9. **Termination clause.** Consider language in the event that one of the individuals wants to terminate the agreement with or without cause and how much notice is required.[90]

While it may not magically address any gaps in long-term care needed, a family care plan can make these more transparent, shedding light on areas where more support is needed and on the work and financial contribution done by those providing the care. In addition, family care plans protect the senior and their family should the need arise to provide the asset documentation required for the Medicaid application. A family care plan formalizes and documents the current situation wherein families are the primary resource to provide care for seniors not eligible for Medicaid. However, as we have explored, this solution frequently results in women's sacrifice as low wage or unpaid caregivers perpetuating a cycle of poverty.

SOLUTION—PACE, MFP AND BUILD BACK BETTER

The political landscape makes it difficult to entertain a comprehensive political solution that would provide a social safety net allowing seniors to age in place—living safely in their homes and communities. Perhaps Joanne Kenen, POLITICO's former health editor, said it best: "The same ideological debates that roil other aspects of health care play a role here, too. How much is a family's responsibility and how much is the government's? How much should the private sector figure out, amid a dysfunctional long-term care insurance market and inadequate benefits and flexibility for employed caregivers?"[91]

However, there are a number of programs which already exist, although they are by no means universally accessible and are also subject to Medicaid eligibility, meaning that seniors must first be bankrupt to be eligible to receive services. PACE (Program of All-Inclusive Care for the Elderly) and MFP (Money Follows the Person) are two publicly funded programs that leverage Medicaid funding to provide an alternative to the traditional Medicaid bed in a skilled nursing facility. The success and challenges of these programs may shed some light on what a comprehensive plan for seniors to age in place could look like should the Biden Build Back Better proposal be funded.

PACE (Program of All-Inclusive Care for the Elderly)

While not universally available, there is an alternative to skilled nursing care funded through Medicaid in thirty states and more than two hundred and seventy locations. The PACE program is designed to keep the frail elderly in their home. The program is free to Medicaid eligible, once again requiring the seniors bankrupt themselves before getting care. However, seniors who are Medicare eligible can buy into the program paying the Medicaid rate of $4,781 per month. While a steep price tag, as of May 2021, on average the cost of care in a skilled nursing facility is *about $275 per day*, according to Genworth's 2020 Cost of Care analysis, or over $8,000 per month.[92]

The National PACE Association writes: "To qualify for PACE, a person must be age 55 or over, live in a PACE service area, and be certified by the state to need a nursing home level care. The typical PACE participant is similar to the average nursing home resident, an 80-year-old woman with eight medical conditions and limitations in three activities of daily living. Nearly half (49 percent) of PACE participants have been diagnosed with dementia. Despite a high level of care needs, more than 90 percent of PACE participants are able to continue to live in their community."[93]

The vision for PACE is to provide a comprehensive and coordinated array of services to keep even the frailest elderly in their home. According to Elligibility.com: "The services included in the PACE program include: adult day care that offers nursing; physical, occupational and recreational therapies; meals; nutritional counseling; social work and personal care; medical care provided by a PACE physician familiar with the history, needs and preferences of each participant; home health care and personal care; all necessary prescription drugs; social services; medical specialties, such as audiology, dentistry, optometry, podiatry and speech therapy; respite care; and hospital and nursing home care when necessary."[94] This comprehensive program of services relies on senior adult day care as the primary vehicle for delivery.

The National PACE Association fact sheet further adds: "PACE utilizes interdisciplinary teams—which include physicians, nurse practitioners, nurses, social workers, therapists, van drivers and aides—to exchange information and solve problems as the conditions and needs of PACE participants change, all with the objective of enabling them to live longer in the community."

As we have explored in previous chapters, the provision of health care and needed social services for seniors is very fragmented. This coordination of services and sharing of information is a key benefit of the PACE program.

PACE participants, although largely a population of frail elderly, have been found to be able to live in their homes and communities on average four years longer than if they had not participated in PACE.[95] The program is working. However, in order to be cost effective, it has to have a sizeable population base in order to efficiently deliver care under the Medicare and Medicaid reimbursement guidelines. To get to that level of efficient and cost-effective care delivery takes upwards of a year for a new program, so States and local governments incur expenses until the scale of the program is fully covered by Medicaid. This has prevented PACE program expansion especially in rural areas.

Until 2015, the PACE program had been administered only by non-profits but looking for ways to expand the program, the Centers for Medicare and Medicaid Services changed the rules to allow for-profit businesses to provide PACE services. With the high incidences of mortality in skilled nursing facilities due to COVID-19, government and health care providers alike took a renewed look at PACE expansion. Democrats in Congress proposed an expansion of the model through the PACE Plus Act, which, if enacted, would allow for the creation of new PACE programs in more states and PACE deserts—and the expansion of current ones—through federal grants, while also offering incentives for non-PACE states to take up the model.

Federal investment in the program has fueled private sector engagement. InnovAge, the largest PACE organization, went public through a $350 million IPO in 2021. "We continue to see positive federal and state legislative activity at levels we have not seen in recent memory," InnovAge CEO Maureen Hewitt said on the company's Q4 earnings call in September 2021. "This is a very encouraging sign for PACE, as interest in the program is at an all-time high." Some PACE providers are already realizing healthy profits. "The average margin monthly per member is over $1,000, Dr. Robert Schreiber, the vice president and medical director of the PACE organization Summit ElderCare."[96]

However, there is concern that for-profits will taint the program's reputation in the same way some for-profits damaged trust in skilled nursing and hospice care. Similarly, critics are wary of some Silicon Valley entrepreneurs who are advocating for a higher dependence on video calls, as opposed to in-person doctor visits because of the COVID-19 pandemic. Assistance with the activities of daily living is, by necessity, a hands-on, in-person experience. Providers are finding that low pay and challenging working conditions are a barrier to hiring and retaining home health workers. This must be addressed in order to ensure that seniors can receive the care they need.

Money Follows the Person

Money Follows the Person is another Medicaid-funded program designed to support seniors to live in their home communities with support. Participating seniors must meet Medicaid eligibility guidelines with its strict income and asset requirements. As of April 2021, thirty-three states participate in Money Follows the Person. The program offers an incentive to the states in the form of federal grants for transition services from a Medicaid-funding nursing home or other institution back into the community, as well as to provide home and community-based services to make the transition successful. Specific to MFP are services and supports that are not generally paid for by Medicaid but make a transition to community living possible. This might include the payment of a security deposit and utility deposits, purchasing furniture for an apartment, covering moving expenses, or even paying for a trial visit to a potential residence in the community. To be clear, MFP does not cover the cost of rent or mortgage.

According to Medicaid studies, "MFP has helped more than 100,000 people move out of institutions and into the community. In addition to helping participants live where they want to live, improving quality of life and preventing re-institutionalization, the program saves significant money for Medicaid programs. During the last year, MFP has become more important than ever. With residents of institutions at particularly high risk of dying from COVID-19, helping people who wish to transition to safer settings in the community has become imperative."[97]Congress has passed five short-term extensions of MFP since funding expired in 2018.[98] The lack of reliable funding has caused states to significantly decrease the number of transitions under this program, with a more than 50 percent decrease between June 2018 and July 2019. A number of states have completely shut down their MFP programs or are in the process of doing so.[99] In December 2020, Congress passed a three-year extension of the program as part of the Consolidated Appropriations Act.

These two programs show that there is a role for government not only in paying for nursing home care, but in supporting seniors to live safely in their home communities with support. However, to-date these programs have not been consistently funded, universally available or available to working or middle-class seniors. Eligibility for these programs has been restricted to seniors who meet the very low income and asset eligibility guidelines for Medicaid assistance.

Seniors who participate in these programs realize life-enhancing benefits, and states realize cost savings. However, the transition to these programs requires state participation and with uncertain federal funding and a period of deficit spending before full capacity is reached, states can opt out of the program or limit enrollment. This is a clear indication that federal funding of options for community-based care is necessary.

Build Back Better

President Biden's Build Back Better agenda includes a significant investment in home care for seniors including seniors who do not meet the strict income and asset tests for Medicaid. While the outcome for this legislation remains uncertain at the time of this writing, the plan includes funding to address many of the challenges for seniors, their families and caregivers outlined in this book. The headwinds that the legislation is facing are the same as those faced by proponents of Medicare in the 1960s and of Medicaid expansion since then. America remains ambivalent, and a portion of the electorate is downright hostile, to government having a role in caring for those who cannot care for themselves including children, the disabled and the elderly.

As we learned in chapter two, our nation has long grappled with the issue of caring for the frail elderly. There is an underlying assumption that the family, specifically wives and daughters, are responsible for care. Thus, today, women make up the overwhelming majority of unpaid and low wage caregivers. Backlash against federal funding for social programs is as old as our nation as well. Funding for these programs which could benefit the working and middle class have long received pushback due to the fear of creating entitlements for the poor. Concessions to establishment conservatives have been at the root of the failure to enact a comprehensive system for senior care. Delegation of the implementation of Medicare and Medicaid to the states allowed for racial segregation of health services to continue. Left to set their own priorities, states continue to shortchange budgets for senior nutrition, home health and other services to support seniors living in their homes.

The Build Back Better agenda is a once in a generation opportunity to change the current system in recognition of the crisis of the growing number of seniors ending their years in poverty, forced into congregant care. Build Back better includes funding for Medicaid expansion to support programs like PACE and Money Follows the Person to expand their availability. In addition, there is funding for programs aimed at those who are not Medicaid eligible—the middle class.

The pending legislation includes funding for tax credits for seniors and caregivers. According to Caring Senior Service: "It proposes as much as $5,000 to help reimburse families for the costs associated with unpaid caregiving. This tax break could help benefit middle-class families who make too much money to qualify for Medicaid but who also don't make enough money to pay for their loved one's long-term care...Biden's plan also includes social security credits for family members who care for their aging loved ones. These credits would help make up for the time they spend out of the workforce to fulfill their caregiving responsibilities." The plan also includes funding for training for caregivers, research to combat chronic diseases including Alzheimer's and diabetes, and the ability to negotiate lower prices on prescription drugs. While not fully funding the cost of senior care, these programs would mark a first step in reducing the costs for families and supporting seniors and their caregivers.

WRAP UP

As a family member looking to determine the optimal living environment for a senior in my care, I wish I had known sooner about the work of Dr. Karen Wilson and her definition of the key attributes for assisted senior living. As families are evaluating solutions, the specificity of the attributes can serve as a checklist or guidelines for evaluating options. The three pillars of housing, healthcare and autonomy are the anchors of any plan and any solution for a dependent senior will need to address all three and navigate any tradeoffs, recognizing that no solution will be perfect because our society does not yet have a comprehensive program to support seniors to age in place in the community.

The solutions proposed in this chapter to address the three key areas are practical ways that families can work together with the senior in their care to maximize the available resources for housing and healthcare while emphasizing autonomy. My diving catch solution of purchasing the little trailer in a senior park and maximizing my mother's limited income to pay for home health aides actually aligned well to the housing and healthcare key attributes. My mother was able to stretch her days living independently with community support for close to two years. Could these precious days have been stretched further?

Had I been successful in obtaining a Financial Power of Attorney perhaps I could have intervened sooner to ensure that her nest egg could stretch. Perhaps if I had negotiated a Family Agreement, perhaps other extended family members could have been more engaged in her care. The technology options in mountainous, rural Placerville were limited, but if I was able to do online shopping and secure some of the home safety assists it would have been a great help. Had my mother made use of Senior Day Care, the hub for delivery of senior services through the PACE program, that could also have made a difference. However, the biggest difference would be if these services were widely available, known, coordinated, regulated, and reasonably priced. For this, we will need comprehensive legislation like what is being proposed in the Build Back Better plan. Families need to advocate at the state and national levels for themselves and for the seniors in their care.

CONCLUSION

While the wealthy can afford care options pushing as much as $10,000 per month, and Medicaid exists for the poor, there are few options for middle class families struggling to support seniors to live safely and with dignity.

As I was finishing the writing of this book, I came across an article in an AARP publication authored by Amy Goyer who is AARP's family and caregiving expert and the author of *Juggling Life, Work and Caregiving*. In her very personal narrative, she walks through the process of how she had to declare bankruptcy after years of caregiving for her aging parents. Amy tells the reader, "I do not need, nor want, sympathy. I do, however, want people to understand the real costs of caregiving. We shouldn't have to make a choice between financial devastation and providing quality care. People are living longer but with chronic health issues. My parents planned for their future but didn't predict their high long-term care costs."[100]

Bankruptcy can be the fate awaiting caregiver and the dependent elderly. The system is designed so that the dependent elderly must actually be bankrupt in order to qualify for Medicaid, which is the only source of public subsidies for long-term care. As we have learned, Medicare does not cover long-term care. There are some limited coverage options available for veterans through the VA and for the few who have long-term care insurance.

Many Boomer women may be at risk of aging into poverty, as we've talked about throughout the book. A Brookings Institute report cites the common reasons for the paucity of women's retirement savings:

- For a variety of reasons, women earn less on average over the course of a lifetime than men do. Lower lifetime earnings make it harder for women to save for retirement. Lower wages and absences from the workforce due to caregiving responsibilities are key factors which result in lower lifetime earnings.

- Women receive Social Security benefits that are, on average, 80 percent of those men receive. Having a first child reduces a woman's Social Security benefits (through reduced earnings) by an average of 16 percent. Each additional child increases the gap by 2 percent. Women who leave work to care for an elderly family member not only lose wages, they also lose an average of $131,000 in lifetime Social Security benefits. Women are more likely to run out of retirement savings, especially because older women are more likely to be the surviving partner, living on less Social Security income and with their partner's medical bills.

- In 2017, among elderly women, the poverty rate was 4.3 percent for those who were married, 13.9 percent for widows, 15.8 percent for divorced women, and 21.5 percent for never married women. More and more women reaching retirement are divorced or unmarried.

- Women still comprise a majority of the estimated 55 million U.S. workers who are not eligible for or covered by an employer-sponsored retirement plan.

- Exacerbating these differences, women are on average longer lived, and live longer with more chronic conditions

- As investors, women are more risk averse, less financially literate. For women who have some retirement savings this is an issue because with the demise of defined benefit pension plans, everyone is responsible for investment decisions for their 401K or IRA retirement accounts.

My mother outlived her savings, depleting it at a rapid rate due to the debilitating effects of diabetes. She was also divorced and a widow, part of the 15.8 percent of the cohort single women who age into poverty. There were other factors that contributed to my mother's financial situation. Although she was a CPA, like many she was not a savvy investor and was swayed by her desire to help relatives and make charitable donations.

My mother also had confidence in the prescribed path that the senior housing industry sells to vulnerable seniors seeking care. She signed up for a pricy independent living apartment thinking that she was doing the right thing for her and for her family. As we know now, she was mistaken.

For seniors and their families, I hope that the solutions provided in this book can serve as a starting place to assist you when faced with what is becoming an all-too-common problem. I scrambled to put supports in place for my mother, all the while thinking that somehow I should be doing more, or that I was missing something. Have faith in yourself and all that you are doing for your loved ones. It's hard, and you're not alone.

Amy Goyer concluded her essay by advising that families get help and seek to maximize all resources and services available. I couldn't agree more.

I'd like to leave you with three lists of things that you can do, no matter where in the aging process you or your family find yourselves. The first is a collection of general takeaways. The second two contain specific advice for family and seniors depending on their financial situations.

GENERAL ADVICE FOR FAMILIES

- Don't believe the marketing. For middle class Americans, understand that what you are seeing on TV may not be a viable option for care for your aging parent. The cost of independent living facilities or live-in, twenty-four-hour caregivers can exceed $100,000 per year and stretch out for years.

- It's okay to wait. While independent living facilities are marketed as attractive alternatives for seniors as young as sixty, delaying a move from the family home is advisable. Look for ways for the senior to receive help at home and get or stay engaged in the community. While independent living facilities may look attractive, and finances may appear stable, a change in health status or a downturn in the economy may draw down funds more rapidly than expected. While earning income may still be possible in the early years of retirement, there are very few options for seniors in their 80s or later.

- Medicare does not cover long-term care. Medicaid does, but it is subject to very low asset restrictions. Other options for funding for long-term care include long-term care insurance and veteran's benefits, though both can have their limitations.

- Understand the trade-offs. While the specific care needs of seniors may vary, the trade-offs are similar. You will need to strike the balance between independence and autonomy, balanced against safety and risk mitigation. And between the ideal level of care and what your resources will cover. You will need to do this on an ongoing basis as needs change over time.

- Prioritize. Focus your financial resources on what is most important, most costly, and where there are limited options for public funding—shelter and medical care. There are programs and charities to help to provide food and cover the cost of basic utilities, but shelter and medical care are costly, and options are limited. Have a plan to cover these items that can adapt over time to adapt to changing needs.

- Have a progression plan. Sometimes a senior moves from one level of care to another quickly or without warning. Be prepared beforehand. Frequently, falls, accidents or bout of illness require quick transitions to an increased level of care.

- Create a system to keep track of important documents like birth and marriage certificates, Social Security cards, bank statements, Social Security statements, insurance bills and coverage information, receipts for medical expenses, utility bills, tax returns. Should the need arise to apply for government assistance, you will need to show eligibility and produce documents supporting need.

- Get other voices involved. Elderly parents may not make decisions that are in their best interest or that we agree with, or which would make our lives easier. They are free to make these decisions. Try to find a trusted influencer who can help a recalcitrant elder understand the pitfalls of their decisions—clergy, trusted family members, attorneys or doctors may be able to help. Work to establish a relationship in advance of a crisis.

- Engage the family in creating a care plan for mom and dad. All family members can contribute some portion of their time, talent, and treasure. Contribution levels may not be equal, but the notion that daughters and daughters-in-law are solely responsible for elder care needs to be challenged. Ideally the care plan should be documented and updated. Putting a plan in writing can bring to light gaps and provide all family members with a view into the financial support and time demands required to provide care.

- Get creative. You may not be able to get ahead of the curve and have a well-resourced plan. COVID-19 and the dramatic drop in the Dow Jones is an example of impacts we could not foresee. While not a perfect solution, buying the trailer was a good solution. Can you get creative in caring for a parent? Create a space in your home? Move into their home? Move to a lower cost location? Barter caregiving for a professional service?

Here's my advice if you're at the beginning of the journey with a senior loved one, while you and the dependent senior may have financial resources still available.

EARLY ADVICE

- Use the framework created by Dr. Keren Wilson as outlined in chapter five to evaluate options for senior living considering the three pillars of housing, healthcare, and autonomy.

- Ensure that a trusted family member or other party has or can get a durable Power of Attorney for Healthcare and that an Advanced Directive is in place. Without these important legal documents, should there be a healthcare emergency, HIPAA laws protecting patient privacy may prevent family members for engaging with healthcare providers and social workers. These documents can be signed at the hospital, but in the event that the senior is incapacitated, it is best to have documents prepared in advance.

- Ideally, seniors should designate a trusted family member or other party to have Financial Power of Attorney. This may be difficult as discussions over money may become contentious or it may be difficult to choose a family member to entrust with mom and dad's financial decision making. There are work arounds. I sat with my mother each month to pay bills and discuss her budget. This could be a starting place. As with any budget, the important part is not only the plan but monitoring the plan to adjust for any changes and to guard against overspending.

- Identify if the senior has a long-term care policy or is eligible for veteran's benefits, what these benefits will cover, how and when to apply, and the process to draw the benefits. Amy Goyer realized fairly late in the process that her parents had a long-term-care policy, and her father was eligible for veteran's benefits. Review the policies so that you are familiar with the eligibility guidelines and any restrictions.

- Look outside of the box for solutions. This could mean building and ADU in the yard to accommodate mom and dad, finding co-housing options, or locating a cost effective senior mobile home park. Review the local requirements for subsidized senior housing so that you know when to apply. Investigate charitable institutions and the VA if a senior is a veteran.

- Create the framework for a family care plan or update the plan you may have already put in place. This plan may need to be modified over time and family members may not all be able to contribute financially, but ideally all could contribute in some way. These can be difficult conversations but are important to uncover gaps that could leave a senior without an important service.

- Document all expenses spent caring for a dependent senior. For caregivers, it is all too easy just to pay what needs to be paid, however, this could put your own financial security at risk. In addition, should the senior need to qualify for Medicaid at some point in the future, the look back period will take into account any undocumented transfer of cash to a family member. If you are paid for your service as a caregiver, keep good records.

- Get seniors comfortable with and using the technology aids which can help to keep them living safely at home—home security devices, medication reminders, automated appliances, fall monitors. In addition to the physical removal of tripping hazards, technology can be a great assist. Socializing, on-line gaming and audio books can be mentally stimulating.

Lastly, I'd like to offer advice if a dependent senior has run out of money, and you find yourself facing even tougher choices.

EMERGENCY ADVICE

- Prioritize housing. If the senior does not medically qualify for a bed in a skilled nursing facility, the first priority must be housing. Keeping the senior in their home, moving into a home of a family member, or finding a low-cost housing solution is key. At this point the senior is eligible for subsidizing housing, but plan for a waiting period of years. It was nearing this point that I bought the trailer in the senior park for my mother.

- Apply for food stamps. Food stamps eligibility can automatically trigger eligibility for other government programs including discounted telephone and internet service and heating and home repair assistance. In addition, money otherwise spent on food can be used for housing and home healthcare. Meals on Wheels can also support seniors to get better nutrition and provide a friendly face for a daily wellness check. The county public benefits office and senior center can help to source government resources.

- Investigate senior day care to get caregiving support. senior day care can be a respite for seniors and their caregivers. Medicaid eligibility can offset the cost and seniors can get a meal, medication, and socialization during the day allowing caregivers to work. Each county is different and Medicaid slots may have a waiting list. Investigate if your community has a PACE program which coordinates care for Medicaid-eligible patients. Senior day care sites often service as the focal point for delivery of services.

- Investigate IHSS. IHSS pays family members to take care of the dependent elderly. The wages are low and there may be a waiting list, but this could provide an income source for family members taking care of a senior in their home. IHSS can also source and pay for non-family member caregivers.

- Medicaid does fund a limited amount of assisted living facilities. Look to get on waiting lists and visit the facilities in your area. Also visit skilled nursing facilities. Should the senior's health condition change, it is helpful to know have visited the facilities in advance. Sometimes hospital discharge planning can be rushed providing no time for an advanced visit.

- Invest in creating community with your dependent senior. My mother's mobile home park had a book and video lending library, a food pantry, an activities center, and held an annual rummage sale. I contributed and participated in these activities and in holiday dinner parties. I got to know the neighbors and spent time in the park.

If you and your parents have worked hard all their lives, you may be shocked to find yourselves in this situation. You may be thinking, "this can't happen to me" or that your parent must have done something wrong. Take solace and remember Amy Goyer's final words of advice: "don't should on yourself."[101] She reminded herself that she did the best she could with the knowledge that she had at the time. I'm confident you did as well.

In addition, we can acknowledge that we have significant gaps in America's institutions and systems designed to care for our dependent elderly. Growing social inequality and a fragmented social safety net allows some Americans to retire in comfort and transfer their assets to their children. For many, that is not the reality. Trusting our retirement nest egg to the vagaries of the stock market and the care for our elders to the investor class leaves us vulnerable to the same fate that awaited my mother—ending her life in poverty.

It does not have to be this way. In a study published in Georgetown University's Journal of Gender and the Law, author Nancy E. Shurtz sums it up well: "One of the principal elements is that contemporary institutions in the United States are based significantly on denial of relationship of dependency in favor of structures founded on presumptions of universal individual autonomy and free association between sovereign actors. Put simply, society functions because we depend on others, but modern institutions are built around the individual."

We have identified practical solutions that individuals and families can take to provide care for the dependent elderly and what steps to take should your mother or father fall into poverty. However, as the large and vocal Boomer generation become the next generation of dependent elderly, political pressure can grow to change the system.

History has shown us that with robust advocacy from citizen's groups, change is possible. Here are several things you can focuses on now and going forward on the advocacy front:

- Expand Medicare and Medicaid to cover paid in-home care. Lower the eligibility age for Medicare and allow Medicare to negotiate prescription drug prices.

- Expand funding for IHSS to boost caregiver wages and clear waiting lists. With enhanced wages can come increased training and support to improve the quality of care.

- Enable paid family leave to care for dependent elderly as well as for children. Currently, twenty-two countries provide paid family leave to care for an adult family member's health needs. Of these, thirteen are completely publicly funded. The remainder are funded through a combination of employer and public funds. No scheme leaves out small employers.

- Provide tax credits for caregivers. One viable measure is to create a $3,000 to $5,000 income-related, refundable tax credit (similar to the existing per child tax credit) available for families helping to care for the chronically ill person as well as support for the Activities of Daily Living. The current credit should be increased to be more comparable to the child credit.

- Expand the Earned Income Tax Credit (EITC) program to include care for an elderly dependent the same as care for children. The EITC provides a tax credit, not a deduction, for low to moderate income workers with dependent children.

- Fund public housing and co-housing for dependent elderly seniors with access to public transportation and health services.

My hope is that in sharing my experience with my mother, we will all be more prepared to help our seniors navigate the challenges of aging in America. While the programs and tools outlined in this book can help individuals and families, as a society we can and must do better by our elders to enable them to live safely at home in the community. Private solutions leave us all in isolation, and privatization monetizes us at every turn. Ultimately, we must work together so that the challenges that my mother faced, and perhaps yours as well, can be addressed by shoring up the gaps in the social services safety net.

Our seniors deserve to age with love, support, and dignity, versus aging into poverty.

NOTES

1. Bureau, US Census. "The Supplemental Poverty Measure: 2017." Census.gov, December 6, 2021. https://www.census.gov/library/publications/2018/demo/p60-265.html.

2. U.S. Assisted Living Facility Market Growth Report, 2021-2027. https://www.grandviewresearch.com/industry-analysis/us-assisted-living-facility-market.

3. Pearson, Caroline F., Wilson KB, Freedman VA, Stevenson DG, Grabowski DC, Coe NB, Watts MO, et al. "The Forgotten Middle: Many Middle-Income Seniors Will Have Insufficient Resources for Housing and Health Care: Health Affairs Journal." Health Affairs, April 24, 2019. https://www.healthaffairs.org/doi/full/10.1377/hlthaff.2018.05233.

4. PricewaterhouseCoopers. "Retirement in America: Time to Rethink and Retool." PwC. https://www.pwc.com/us/en/industries/asset-wealth-management/library/retirement-in-america.html.

5. "Consumer Prices up 8.5 Percent for Year Ended March 2022." U.S. Bureau of Labor Statistics. U.S. Bureau of Labor Statistics, April 18, 2022. https://www.bls.gov/opub/ted/2022/consumer-prices-up-8-5-percent-for-year-ended-march-2022.htm.

6. "Your Guide to Medicare and Rehabilitation Services." Kindred. https://www.kindredhealthcare.com/resources/blog-kindred-spirit/2018/09/13/your-guide-to-medicare-and-rehabilitation-services.

7. Wagner, David. Poorhouse America's Forgotten Institution. New York: Gotham Books, 2022.

8. Ruggles, Steven. "Multigenerational Families in Nineteenth-Century America." https://users.pop.umn.edu/~ruggles/multigenerational.pdf.

9. Kaktins, Mara. "Almshouses (Poorhouses)." Encyclopedia of Greater Philadelphia, February 26, 2022. https://philadelphiaencyclopedia.org/essays/almshouses-poorhouses/.

10. "Life and Death in The Antebellum Era 1800—1850." Legacy.com. http://www.legacy.com/life-and-death/the-antebellum-era.html.

11. Genovese, E. D. (1974). Roll Jordan roll: The world the slaves made. New York: Pantheon Books. [See especially pp. 519–523.]

12. "A History of Elder Care." Bayview Healthcare St. Augustine, August 25, 2015. https://www.bayviewhealthcare.org/a-history-of-elder-care/.

13. "The History of Nursing Homes in America." Rincon Del

Rio, August 14, 2021. https://rincondelrio.com/2017/06/18/
the-history-of-nursing-homes-from-almshouses-to-skilled-nursing/.

14. "Edgefield Hotel—McMenamins." https://www.mcmenamins.com/edgefield/
discover/history.

15. Costa, Dora L. "Pensions and Retirement among Black Union Army Veterans."
The journal of economic history. U.S. National Library of Medicine, September
2010. https://www.ncbi.nlm.nih.gov/pmc/articles/PMC3004158/.

16. Khazan, Olga. "What American Healthcare Can Learn from
Germany." The Atlantic. Atlantic Media Company, April
8, 2014. https://www.theatlantic.com/health/archive/2014/04/
what-american-healthcare-can-learn-from-germany/360133/.

17. Carol. "The History of Nursing Homes in America." Rincon
Del Rio, August 14, 2021. https://rincondelrio.com/2017/06/18/
the-history-of-nursing-homes-from-almshouses-to-skilled-nursing/.

18. Gauthier, Jason, History Staff. "Urban and Rural Areas—History—U.S. Census
Bureau." United States Census Bureau. https://www.census.gov/history/www/
programs/geography/urban_and_rural_areas.html.

19. Hoyt, Jeff. "Senior Living History: 1900—1929." SeniorLiving.org, August 10,
2021. https://www.seniorliving.org/history/1900-1929/.

20. "The History of Nursing Homes in America." Rincon Del
Rio, August 14, 2021. https://rincondelrio.com/2017/06/18/
the-history-of-nursing-homes-from-almshouses-to-skilled-nursing/.

21. "Timeline: A History of Elder Care in America," Al Jazeera America, accessed
April 26, 2022, http://america.aljazeera.com/watch/shows/america-tonight/
america-tonight-blog/2014/2/25/history-elderly-care.html.

22. "Edgefield Hotel—McMenamins." demo. Accessed March 24, 2022. https://
www.mcmenamins.com/edgefield/discover/history.

23. Hoyt, Jeff. "Senior Living History: 1930—1939." SeniorLiving.org, August 10,
2021. https://www.seniorliving.org/history/1930-1939/.

24. Lee, Nathaniel. "How 401(k) Accounts Killed Pensions to Become One of the
Most Popular Retirement Plans for U.S. Workers." CNBC. CNBC, March 24,
2021. https://www.cnbc.com/2021/03/24/how-401k-brought-about-the-death-
of-pensions.html.

25. Morrissey, Monique. "The State of American Retirement: How 401(k)s Have
Failed Most American Workers." Economic Policy Institute. https://www.epi.org/
publication/retirement-in-america/.

26. "Gender Financial Gap Massive in 401K Balances—401K …". 401K
Specialist Magazine. June 25, 2019. https://401kspecialistmag.com/
gender-financial-gap-massive-in-401k-balances/.

27. Hoyt, Jeff. "Senior Living History: 1940—1949." SeniorLiving.org, April 27, 2021. https://www.seniorliving.org/history/1940-1949/.

28. Eldred, Sheila Mulrooney. "When Harry Truman Pushed for Universal Health Care." History.com. A&E Television Networks, November 12, 2019. https://www.history.com/news/harry-truman-universal-health-care.

29. Hoyt, Jeff. "Senior Living History: 1960—1969." SeniorLiving.org, August 10, 2021. https://www.seniorliving.org/history/1960-1969/.

30. Mendelson, Mary Adelaide. Tender Loving Greed: How the Incredibly Lucrative Nursing Home "Industry" Is Exploiting America's Old People and Defrandings Us All. New York: Vintage Books, 1975.

31. "Welltower Expands Sunrise Senior Living Relationship with Purchase of Five Premier Urban Properties." Welltower Expands Sunrise Senior Living Relationship with Purchase of Five Premier Urban Properties, July 31, 2019. https://www.prnewswire.com/news-releases/welltower-expands-sunrise-senior-living-relationship-with-purchase-of-five-premier-urban-properties-300894340.html.

32. Fund, Colorado Wealth Management. "How Senior Housing Infected Healthcare Reits." SeekingAlpha. Seeking Alpha, March 18, 2020. https://seekingalpha.com/article/4332328-how-senior-housing-infected-healthcare-reits.

33. Slavinsky, Cheryl. "Sunrise Senior Living Reduces Staff Turnover and Costs through Arena's AI Tool." Senior Living News, February 4, 2019. https://www.seniorlivingnews.com/sunrise-senior-living-reduces-staff-turnover-and-costs-through-arenas-ai-tool/.

34. Gerace, Alyssa. "Sunrise CEO Earns $16.8 Million Compensation for Turnaround Success." Senior Housing News, December 10, 2012. https://seniorhousingnews.com/2012/12/10/sunrise-ceo-earns-16-8-million-compensation-for-turnaround-success/.

35. "Tax Reform Is a Windfall for REIT Investors." Yahoo! News. Yahoo!. April, 13 2018. https://www.yahoo.com/news/tax-reform-windfall-reit-investors-134413034.html.

36. Sudo, Chuck. "Welltower CEO: Coronavirus Outbreak Could Show Value of Senior Care Communities." Senior Housing News, March 2, 2020. https://seniorhousingnews.com/2020/03/02/welltower-ceo-coronavirus-outbreak-could-show-value-of-senior-care-communities/.

37. "Medicare Advantage in 2021: Enrollment Update and Key Trends." KFF, June 24, 2021. https://www.kff.org/medicare/issue-brief/medicare-advantage-in-2021-enrollment-update-and-key-trends/.

38. Japsen, Bruce. "Humana to Invest $1 Billion in Medicare Advantage Business after Enrollment Comes up Short." Forbes. Forbes Magazine, February 3, 2022. https://www.forbes.com/sites/brucejapsen/2022/02/02/

humana-to-invest-1-billion-in-medicare-advantage-business-after-enrollment-comes-up-short/?sh=525b5661543f.

39. "How Much Care Will You Need?" | ACL Administration for Community Living. https://acl.gov/ltc/basic-needs/how-much-care-will-you-need#:~:text=Someone%20turning%20age%2065%20today,for%20longer%20than%205%20years.

40. Pearson, Caroline F., Wilson KB, Freedman VA, Stevenson DG, Grabowski DC, Coe NB, Watts MO, et al. "The Forgotten Middle: Many Middle-Income Seniors Will Have Insufficient Resources for Housing and Health Care: Health Affairs Journal." Health Affairs, April 24, 2019. https://www.healthaffairs.org/doi/full/10.1377/hlthaff.2018.05233.

41. Shurtz, Nancy E. "Long-Term Care and the Tax Code: A Feminist Perspective." https://www.law.georgetown.edu/gender-journal/wp-content/uploads/sites/20/2019/01/GT-GJGL180036.pdf.

42. National Center on Caregiving at Family Caregiver Alliance. "Women and Caregiving: Facts and Figures." https://www.caregiver.org/resource/women-and-caregiving-facts-and-figures/.

43. Kunkle, Fredrick. "Daughters Tend to Aging Parents More Often than Sons, but Some Are Seeking a Change." The Washington Post. WP Company, December 5, 2014. https://www.washingtonpost.com/local/daughters-tend-to-aging-parents-more-often-than-sons-but-some-are-seeking-a-change/2014/12/05/b593f554-74ee-11e4-9d9b-86d397daad27_story.html.

44. Rosenberg, Alyssa. "Five New Movies Explain Why Caregiving Is Real Work." The Washington Post. WP Company, October 26, 2021. https://www.washingtonpost.com/news/act-four/wp/2014/09/17/five-new-movies-explain-why-caregiving-is-real-work/.

45. "Baby Boomers as Caregivers: Results from the Behavioral Risk Factor Surveillance System in 44 States, the District of Columbia, and Puerto Rico, 2015–2017." Centers for Disease Control and Prevention. Centers for Disease Control and Prevention, August 13, 2020. https://www.cdc.gov/pcd/issues/2020/20_0010.htm.

46. Kerr, Nancy. "Family Caregivers Experience High out-of-Pocket Costs." AARP, June 29, 2021. https://www.aarp.org/caregiving/financial-legal/info-2021/high-out-of-pocket-costs/?cmp=RDRCT-867fa361-20211014.

47. Shurtz, Nancy E. "Long-Term Care and the Tax Code: A Feminist Perspective." https://www.law.georgetown.edu/gender-journal/wp-content/uploads/sites/20/2019/01/GT-GJGL180036.pdf.

48. "Home Care Aides At A Glance," February 2014. https://phinational.org/wp-content/uploads/legacy/phi-facts-5.pdf.

49. Hanson, Ginger C, Nancy A Perrin, Helen Moss, Naima Laharnar, and Nancy

Glass. "Workplace Violence against Homecare Workers and Its Relationship with Workers Health Outcomes: A Cross-Sectional Study." BMC public health. BioMed Central, January 17, 2015. https://www.ncbi.nlm.nih.gov/pmc/articles/PMC4308913/.

50. Span, Paula. "For Older Adults, Home Care Has Become Harder to Find." The New York Times. The New York Times, July 24, 2021. https://www.nytimes.com/2021/07/24/health/coronavirus-elderly-home-care.html.

51. El Dorado County In-Home Supportive Services. 2016 Annual Report. https://www.edcgov.us/Government/HumanServices/Protective%20Services/IHSS%20Public%20Authority/documents/PA%20IHSS%20AC%20Annual%20Report%20FY%2015-16%20FINAL.pdf.

52. Robin Rudowitz Follow @RRudowitz on Twitter, Elizabeth Williams Follow @Liz_Williams_ on Twitter. "Medicaid Financing: The Basics." KFF, May 7, 2021. https://www.kff.org/medicaid/issue-brief/medicaid-financing-the-basics/view/print/.

53. "Analysis of the Human Services Budget." The 2017-18 Budget: Analysis of the Human Services Budget, February 28, 2017. https://lao.ca.gov/Publications/Report/3576/2.

54. Horseman, Jeff. "Why in-Home Care for California's Needy Could Strain County Budgets." Daily News. Daily News, August 28, 2017. https://www.dailynews.com/2017/04/09/why-in-home-care-for-californias-needy-could-strain-county-budgets/.

55. "Considering the State Costs and Benefits: In-Home Supportive Services Program." Considering the state costs and benefits: In-home supportive services program, January 21, 2010. https://lao.ca.gov/reports/2010/ssrv/ihss/ihss_012110.aspx.

56. "Easy Targets: How California's IHSS Program Endangers People with Disabilities • Free Wheelin'." Free Wheelin', June 6, 2017. https://www.freewheelintravel.org/ihsscalifornia/.

57. Abrams, Abigail. "Democrats Want to Reform This Program That Helps Poor Elderly and Disabled Americans." Democrats want to reform this program that helps poor elderly and disabled Americans, July 22, 2021. https://www.msn.com/en-us/news/politics/democrats-want-to-reform-this-program-that-helps-poor-elderly-and-disabled-americans/ar-AAMrMNa?ocid=msedgntp.

58. "What We Deliver: Meals on Wheels America." What We Deliver | Meals on Wheels America. Accessed January 28, 2022. https://www.mealsonwheelsamerica.org/learn-more/what-we-deliver.

59. COVID "Statement on President's Fiscal Year 2020 Budget." STATEMENT ON PRESIDENT'S FISCAL YEAR 2020 BUDGET. https://www.

mealsonwheelsamerica.org/learn-more/national/press-room/news/2019/03/11/statement-on-president-s-fiscal-year-2020-budget.

60. Paul, Kari. "1 In 10 Senior Households Relies on Food Stamps." MarketWatch. MarketWatch, November 4, 2018. https://www.marketwatch.com/story/1-in-10-senior-households-relies-on-food-stamps-2018-11-02.

61. "7 Facts About Older Adults and SNAP." The National Council on Aging. Accessed January 28, 2022. https://www.ncoa.org/article/7-facts-about-older-adults-and-snap.

62. "7 Facts About Older Adults and SNAP." The National Council on Aging. Accessed January 28, 2022. https://www.ncoa.org/article/7-facts-about-older-adults-and-snap.

63. Godoy, Maria. "Judge Blocks Rule That Would Have Kicked 700,000 People off Snap." NPR. NPR, March 14, 2020. https://www.npr.org/sections/thesalt/2020/03/14/815748914/judge-blocks-rule-that-would-have-kicked-700-000-people-off-snap.

64. Bennett, Jared, and Ashley Wong. "Millions of Poor Lose Access to Cellphone Service under Trump Administration Reforms." USA Today. Gannett Satellite Information Network, November 7, 2019. https://www.usatoday.com/story/news/investigations/2019/11/05/under-trump-millions-poor-lose-cellphone-service/2482112001/.

65. "Considering the State Costs and Benefits: In-Home Supportive Services Program." Considering the state costs and benefits: In-home supportive services program, January 21, 2010. https://lao.ca.gov/reports/2010/ssrv/ihss/ihss_012110.aspx.

66. Keren Brown Wilson, PhD, Historical Evolution of Assisted Living in the United States, 1979 to the Present, *The Gerontologist*, Volume 47, Issue suppl_1, December 2007, Pages 8–22, https://doi.org/10.1093/geront/47.Supplement_1.8

67. Ibid. Wilson.

68. Keren Brown Wilson, PhD, Historical Evolution of Assisted Living in the United States, 1979 to the Present, *The Gerontologist*, Volume 47, Issue suppl_1, December 2007, Pages 8–22, https://doi.org/10.1093/geront/47.Supplement_1.8

69. James Leggate, "The Villages, Florida, Was Fastest-Growing Metro Area This Decade: Census Bureau," Fox Business (Fox Business, August 12, 2021), https://www.foxbusiness.com/real-estate/the-villages-florida-fastest-growing-metro-area-decade-census-bureau.

70. Singletary, Michelle. "Who's Living under Your Roof? Why a Multigenerational Household Can Strengthen Your Family Finances and Bonds." The Washington Post. WP Company, September 18, 2018. https://www.washingtonpost.com/business/2018/09/18/whos-living-under-your-roof-why-mutigenerational-household-can-strengthen-your-family-finances-bonds/.

71. Penn, Ben, and Alex Ruoff. "Democrats Seek to Advance Biden Home-Care Plan via Medicaid Cash." Bloomberg Law, June 23, 2021. https://news.bloomberglaw.com/daily-labor-report/ democrats-set-to-unveil-bill-to-implement-bidens-home-care-plan.

72. Clark, Dea. "New Concept to See Older Women Living Together to Avoid Homelessness, Loneliness." ABC News. ABC News, July 23, 2021. https:// www.abc.net.au/news/2021-07-24/older-women-look-to-live-together-to-avoid-homelessness/100319352?utm_source=abc_news_web&utm_medium=content_shared&utm_campaign=abc_news_web.

73. Sudo, Chuck. "Why Co-Op Senior Housing Is Ready for Primetime." Senior Housing News, September 5, 2019. https://seniorhousingnews.com/2019/09/05/ co-op-senior-housing-starts-to-compete-for-bigger-market-share/.

74. "Cooperative Living." Cooperative Living at Garden Spot Village. Accessed April 24, 2022. https://www.gardenspotvillage.org/residential-choices/ cooperative-living/.

75. Ibid. Wilson.

76. Ibid. Wilson.

77. Kakulla, Brittne Nelson. "2020 Tech Trends of the 50+." AARP, January 1, 2020. https://www.aarp.org/research/topics/technology/info-2019/2020-technology-trends-older-americans.html.

78. Etkin, Keren. "Who Is Investing in the AgeTech Revolution in 2021?" TheGerontechnologist. Publisher Name TheGerontechnologist. com, January 13, 2022. https://www.thegerontechnologist.com/ who-is-investing-in-the-age-tech-revolution/.

79. Ibid. Kakulla, AARP.

80. Gregory, Nicole. "Are Medical Alert Systems Covered by Medicare?" Forbes. Forbes Magazine, March 30, 2022. https://www.forbes.com/health/ healthy-aging/medical-alert-systems-medicare/.

81. "5 Helpful Elderly Monitoring Devices." A Place for Mom, April 16, 2018. https://www.aplaceformom.com/caregiver-resources/articles/ senior-monitoring-sensors.

82. D'Aquila, Mario. "6 Top Tech Products to Help Seniors Age in Place." HomeCare Magazine,

83. Abrahms, Sally. "Technology, Gadgets for Seniors Aging in Place." AARP, March 1, 2014. https://www.aarp.org/home-family/personal-technology/info-2014/ is-this-the-end-of-the-nursing-home.html.

84. Ibid. Abrahms, AARP.

85. "Report: 22 Million U.S. Seniors Lack Broadband Internet Access; First Time

Study Quantifies Digital Isolation of Older Americans as Pandemic Continues to Ravage Nation." Business Wire, January 27, 2021. https://www.businesswire. com/news/home/20210127005243/en/Report-22-Million-U.S.-Seniors-Lack-Broadband-Internet-Access-First-Time-Study-Quantifies-Digital-Isolation-of-Older-Americans-as-Pandemic-Continues-to-Ravage-Nation.

86. "Exposing the Hidden Connectivity Crisis for Older ...—Oats." https://oats. org/wp-content/uploads/2021/01/Aging-Connected-Exposing-the-Hidden-Connectivity-Crisis-for-Older-Adults.pdf.

87. Kurani, Nisha, Nisha Kurani, Jared Ortaliza, Emma Wager Twitter, Lucas Fox, and Krutika Amin Twitter. "How Has U.S. Spending on Healthcare Changed over Time?" Peterson-KFF Health System Tracker, February 25, 2022. https://www.healthsystemtracker.org/ chart-collection/u-s-spending-healthcare-changed-time/.

88. Academic.oup.com. https://academic.oup.com/view-large/131021841.

89. Marshall, Jeffrey, and Tammy Weber. "Children Held Liable for Parents Nursing Home Bills in North Dakota Case—Marshall, Parker & Weber." Marshall Parker Weber, October 15, 2013. https://www.paelderlaw.com/estate-planning/ children-held-liable-for-parents-nursing-home-bills-in-north-dakota-case/.

90. ABA

91. politico

92. Witt, Scott, and Jeff Hoyt. "Skilled Nursing Costs: Average Cost of Skilled Nursing Facilities in 2022." SeniorLiving.org, January 4, 2022. https://www. seniorliving.org/skilled-nursing/cost/.

93. "Eligibility Requirements for Programs of All-Inclusive Care for the Elderly (PACE®): National Pace Association." Eligibility Requirements for Programs of All-Inclusive Care for the Elderly (PACE®) | National PACE Association. https://www.npaonline.org/pace-you/ eligibility-requirements-programs-all-inclusive-care-elderly-pace%C2%AE.

94. Kathryn Anne Stewart. "Medicare Pace Program: How It Works and How to Qualify." Eligibility, June 30, 2020. https://eligibility.com/medicare/ medicare-pace-program.

95. J;, Gyurmey T;Kwiatkowski. "Program of All-Inclusive Care for the Elderly (PACE): Integrating Health and Social Care since 1973." Rhode Island medical journal (2013). U.S. National Library of Medicine. https://pubmed.ncbi.nlm.nih. gov/31167525/.

96. Donlan, Andrew. "Innovage CEO Maureen Hewitt: Pace Tailwinds Stronger than Ever." Home Health Care News, September 22, 2021. https://homehealthcarenews.com/2021/09/ innovage-ceo-maureen-hewitt-pace-tailwinds-stronger-than-ever/.

97. "Money Follows the Person." Money Follows the Person—Protect Our Medicaid. https://medicaid.publicrep.org/feature/money-follows-the-person/.

98. "What Is the Money Follows the Person Demonstration?" https://heller.brandeis.edu/community-living-policy/images/pdfpublications/2020maymfpbrief.pdf.

99. "www.medicaid.gov." https://www.medicaid.gov/sites/default/files/2019-12/teft-evaluationfinal-report.pdf.

100. Goyer, Amy. "How My Family Caregiving Expenses Led to Bankruptcy." AARP, February 26, 2021. https://www.aarp.org/caregiving/financial-legal/info-2021/expenses-financial-strain.html.

101. Ibid. Goyer.

ACKNOWLEDGEMENTS

I would first like to acknowledge my mother, Mary Mulhall, who gave me the opportunity to be her caregiver and most importantly her daughter. I also want to thank the women who shared the role of caregiver with me—Amanda Scott and Sue Kupihea. Your loving care for my mother extended and enriched her life. Michelle E. Smith, my mother's neighbor, did so much for her and for the community at the trailer park. Kacey Carpenter and my children Emma and Kevin Sharp made my work lighter helping me to care for grandma and delighted her with their many visits and kindnesses. Thank you also to Mi Mae Ching who helped me to navigate work while caring for my mother.

As a first-time author, I could not have done this without the skill and support of my editor Gregory Newton Brown. I am honored that he accepted this project and for his encouragement along the way. I would also like to thank Steve Kuhn, whose eye for design made the book come together. Thank you to the scholars whose work is fundamental to this book, Professor David Wagner, author of the Poorhouse, and Dr. Keren Wilson.

ABOUT THE AUTHOR

Kathy Sharp draws on her M.A from Stanford University in Education, her technology background, and her experience in managing federally funded programs to create a compelling work, rich with personal narrative, honest emotion, and extensive policy and services detail.

A native Californian, Kathy now lives outside of Portland, Oregon, and is working to combat hunger with the Portland Fruit Tree Project, Hunger Fighters Oregon and the Association of Gleaning Organizations.